Marketing Mastery:

The Ultimate Guide To Internet & Content Marketing. Drive Demand, Build a Brand, Maximize Traffic, Earn Passive Income and Sell Almost Anything

Copyright Notice

Disclaimer

Claim This Now

The Ultimate Guide to Make Money Onlines

Grab your chance to own this comprehensive two audiobook bundle by Max Lane, covering everything you need to know about how to make money online and passive income ideas.

Including:

- *Make Money Online: Twelve Proven Methods to Earn Passive Income and Work from Anywhere in the World*
- *The Fastlane to Make Money Online: How to Write a Book and Make Passive Income with Self Publishing, Audiobooks and More*

Do you want to learn how to make money online consistently? Without a lot of fuss, scams, or investing any money?

If so - you've come to the right place....

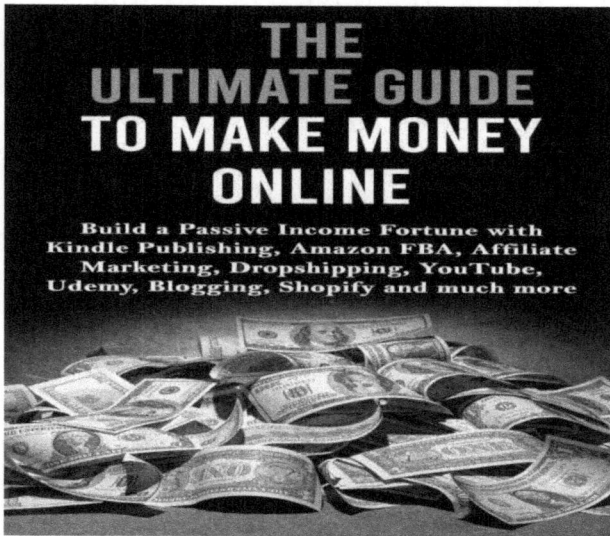

THE ULTIMATE GUIDE TO MAKE MONEY ONLINE

Build a Passive Income Fortune with Kindle Publishing, Amazon FBA, Affiliate Marketing, Dropshipping, YouTube, Udemy, Blogging, Shopify and much more

FREE! Report reveals our most popular article headlines for driving traffic and attracting readers!

Find Out More

Internet Marketing:

Grow Your Business, Build a Brand, Make Money Online and Sell Almost Anything!

Table of Contents

Introduction:
Now Is the Time to Cash In

If you are thinking about starting a business, you should consider setting up an internet marketing business. In this digital age wherein almost anything can be sold through the internet, the opportunities out there are endless. It's definitely easier to build a successful online business than a traditional business. A traditional business comes with a lot of responsibilities which are absent in an online business. For example, if you run an online business, you don't need to worry about rental expenses, utilities expenses, or heavy overhead costs. Everything is online, in the virtual space.

Another great reason why now is the time to start an internet marketing business is the fact that the web offers tons of tools and resources that you can utilize. Not only that but often for free. For instance, you have access to immensely popular networking sites like Facebook, Twitter, and Instagram. These are sites that are free to use and attract billions of users. Chances are your target customers are active in these sites. You can reach these potential customers by merely being active on social media. Free social sites are just the tip of the iceberg. There are other tools, resources, and platforms online that you can use as leverage in building and growing your internet marketing business.

Here's what you should always keep in mind. The internet is a low-cost tool that you can use to market and sell almost anything. It doesn't matter if you are selling a service or a manufactured product. The methods of promoting your goods are pretty much the same. And you have access to a global marketplace. You can choose to sell your goods to anyone. That customer can be a student in Melbourne, Australia or a farmer in Scotland. It's even easier if you are selling a digital product. One that you can deliver to a customer remotely through the internet (i.e. downloadable ebooks and software).

Anyone can start an internet marketing business. There are no qualifications or prior experience required. Don't have a college degree? No problem. A huge number of successful online entrepreneurs didn't even finish high school. Don't have any experience in computer programming? No problem. You don't need to be a technical genius to create a successful business website. The point here is that there are very little barriers to building a successful online business. If you work smart, you can achieve all your business goals. The information is all here for you to discover.

You can even choose to run your internet marketing business as a part-time operation. That means you don't have to leave your main job. You can always work on your online business in your free time. That's the beauty of online entrepreneurship. You own your time. You can work on your business only when you have to. No one is forcing you to wake up at 6:00 am and work until 5:00 pm. You are your own boss, basically.

Building a successful online business is 100% achievable. However, for that to happen, you need to start properly. Starting properly means you must have the resources and the knowledge to make sure that you are heading in the right direction. That's the reason why I've written this book you are currently reading. I'm here to help you get started in the right direction.

In this book, you are going to learn about the basics of internet marketing. I'm going to provide you with all the necessary information you need to start, build, grow, and scale a successful internet marketing business. After reading this book, you should be more than equipped to start a business and grow it to the levels you want. Think of this book as your ultimate guide in your entrepreneurial journey. Let's get going.

Chapter 1:
How to Recognize Your Target Market

This is where the journey begins. You can't start an online business without identifying who your customers will be. You may have the best product or service idea but this amounts to nothing if there's no viable market for it.

With that said, don't build a business around a product or service if you haven't done your market research. Doing market research isn't that difficult. Again, there are many tools and resources online that you can use as leverage for your market research. Most of these tools and resources are also free to use. Make use of tools such as Google trends to identify what is hot online now. Then make use of Google keywords to zoom in on profitable keywords and terms.

Market research can be a complicated process depending on the nature of the business you have in mind. However, allow me to simplify the process. There are six major steps in the market research process. These are as follows:

1. Define your target customer and his/her persona.
2. Understand the characteristics, challenges, and buying habits of your target customer.
3. Engage your target customers to learn from them.
4. Come up with research questions that you can ask your target customers.
5. List and understand your potential competitors.

6. Summarize your research findings.
7. Answer the following question based on your research findings:
Is there a profitable market for your product or service idea?

Let's discuss these steps in more detail.

1. Define your target customer and his/her persona.

You must first understand who your target customers are. As I have mentioned earlier, don't just pursue a business idea because you think that there will be buyers for your product or service. So many would be entrepreneurs have this great idea but without testing it your risking losing time and money.

First off you have to test the idea if it's viable. But how exactly are you going to do that? This is the beginning of your market research. The first thing you should do is write down a quick list of who you think your customers will be. For example, let's say that you have written a tutorial ebook about woodworking. Just off the top of your head, who are the people you think would be interested in purchasing your ebook?

You can list down carpenters, furniture creators, interior decorators, artists, woodworking students, arts and crafts students, and stay-at-home dads as your target market. This is pretty obvious because these are the people who are most likely in need of a guide book about woodworking. They represent those who will likely find value in what you have written in the book. Go over the list a few times to make sure that you have written down all those who would be interested in your product or service.

2. Understand the characteristics, challenges, and buying habits of your target customer.

Now that you have an idea of who your target customers are, the next step is to perform what is referred to as secondary research. In this step, you are going to attempt to verify if your instincts are right. Were you correct in assuming that the people in the list you made will be interested in buying your product or service? In this step, you are no longer going to rely on your instincts. You need to take your market research further by using tools and resources to gather data about your target market.

Remember that your goal here is to identify the characteristics, challenges, and buying habits of your potential customers. This means that you need to collect data about all of these factors. One of the most important tools you can use is a keyword research tool. There are dozens of these tools online. Some are free to use and some are subscription-based. If you are just starting out, I highly recommend that you make use of Google's own keyword research tool. It's 100% free to use. It's very comprehensive. And it offers the most accurate data. That is of course expected given the fact that Google commands more than 60% of online searches.

A keyword research tool helps you understand your potential customers. Where are they coming from? What words and phrases are they using to look for your products and services? What demographics do they belong to? These are just some of the important questions that you can find answers to using a keyword research tool.

3. Engage your target customers to learn from them.

If you have performed step 1 and 2, then you have a clear idea of who your customers are and where they are coming from. What you are going to do next is to engage your potential customers to further learn about them and their needs. Identify the places online where they congregate and hang out. You then get inside these platforms and be among them. Such platforms include social media sites (i.e. Facebook, Twitter, YouTube, and Instagram), blogs, and forums.

Let's take Facebook for example. The social networking site has the Groups feature where people who share the same interests can join and interact in a group page. What you do is find group pages that are very relevant to your product or service, join the pages, and engage with the members. You can learn a lot by simply browsing through the posts and comments in the pages. What topics are they talking about? What products and services are often mentioned in the discussions? As you go through the discussions, make notes of the important details about your target customers.

4. Come up with research questions that you can ask your target customers.

This step involves writing down questions or creating surveys and convincing your potential customers to answer them. There are two ways on how you can do surveys. You can do the surveys yourself or you can outsource the process to a survey company. There are so many of these survey companies around today. However, some survey companies are notorious for using unviable respondents which will obviously lead to misleading data. With that said, I recommend that you perform the surveys yourself. For decent results, you don't have to gather a ton of respondents.

5. List and understand your potential competitors.

You also need to understand your competition. This is something that a lot of new online entrepreneurs often take for granted. Having a high-quality product or service does not guarantee online success. You may have a great product but what if there are hundreds of other great products out there that are very similar to yours? Or if you are competing with huge brands and personalities. The general rule in starting an online business is that you should only enter a particular niche or industry if you are confident that you can compete in the arena.

This is why it's very important that you do competitor research. How tough is the competition in the niche you are targeting? Are you up against established brands or corporations? Are you up against small business operations? Can you offer a product or service that is much better or more affordable compared to the competition? These are some of the questions you should ask yourself when reviewing your competition. Your main goal in researching about your competition is to determine if you can compete against them should you decide to pursue your business idea.

6. Summarize your research findings.
If you have accomplished all of the previous steps, you should have in front of you a mountain of data that pertain to your target market and potential competitors. The next obvious step is to go through all your findings and data and summarize the information so that you can take the proper actions. If you have done your research properly, it shouldn't be that hard to draw clear and actionable conclusions from the information you have gathered.

It's best to put your summary into writing so that you can go over it and review it whenever it's necessary. Keep in mind that the summary of your research findings form the foundation upon which you are going to decide whether it's viable to pursue your business idea or not. Make sure that your summary stays true to the findings of your research.

7. Answer the following question based on your research findings: Is there a profitable market for your product or service idea?
This is it. This is where you finally decide if there's a market for your proposed product or service. After doing the market research, collecting data, organizing your findings, and writing down a summary of your findings, you now have to decide if the idea can be turned into a profitable business. Is there a market for the product or service? The answer should be a "yes" before you can move forward. If it's a "no", then you need to start from the bottom.

The whole point of this chapter is that it's very important to conduct market research before you decide to pursue a business idea. You have to be sure that there are people who will be interested in buying your product or service. The only way for you to know this is to conduct a thorough market research.

Chapter 2:
Understanding the Brand
That You Want To Build

There was a time when the words "brand" and
"branding" were associated with major companies and
multi-million dollar corporations. When people spoke
of brands, they spoke about the likes of Nike or
Colgate or Nestle or Ford Motors. Those days are over.
Thanks to technology and the coming of the digital
age, you don't have to be a multi-million company to
be considered a brand. Small and medium-sized
businesses now have the chance to build their own
brands and compete with major corporations. This is
one of the biggest reasons why there's a growing
number of online entrepreneurs. Today, even a single
person can be considered a brand. If you have a
sizable following online, you are considered a brand.
That's how powerful online marketing can be.

Anyway, since we are talking about internet marketing
businesses here, let's talk about how you can
transform your business idea into a successful brand.
Again, we need to remind you that branding these
days no longer requires a lot of money. Branding is no
longer about purchasing expensive ads in television or
erecting giant billboards or hiring celebrity brand
ambassadors. You have to get rid of this notion that
you are going to need a ton of cash in order to
successfully build a brand.

Online branding is a completely different ball game.
What you need is a good product or service and a
practical branding strategy. Basically, online branding

is about using tools and resources available in the internet with the aim of positioning your brand in a specific marketplace. For example, let's say that you are selling an app that creates digital calendars and schedules for people who want to organize their time. Branding your app entails creating enough hype and online chatter so that when people talk about apps for calendars and schedules, they will be talking about you. They will be talking about your brand in the same sense that consumers talk about Colgate when they discuss about toothpaste products.

In a nutshell, branding is a very powerful technique and you should be spending a good amount of your time and resources on it if you want your online business to be successful. Building your online brand isn't going to be easy. That's something you should expect especially if you are entering a competitive niche where there's a lot of already established brands. Growing your brand is also going to take some time so you need to be patient. You can't build a successful brand overnight.

Before you begin with your online branding campaign, you must have a clear understanding of what type of brand you want to pursue. You have to define the persona or culture that you want to present to customers. For example, The North Face brands itself as an outdoors company that is adventurous and is a risk-taker. Patagonia, on the other hand, brands itself as an outdoors company that is socially-responsible by donating a portion of its profits to environmental causes. LinkedIn brands itself as the social networking site for professionals and entrepreneurs.

The bottomline here is that you must have a branding goal. How do you want your customers to perceive you? It's a lot easier to implement a branding campaign if you and your team clearly understand your branding goals.

Here are some of the most effective ways on how you can grow your online brand:

1. Create a branding theme for all your online operations and activities.
Everything you do that is related to your online business should have some form of cohesiveness. Creating a branding theme is a rather broad term but it basically means doing all things with your branding goals in mind. For example, if you want your consumers to perceive you as a fun and carefree business, then all of your marketing and promotional efforts should be fun, light-hearted, and humorous. Furthermore, you should not forget details like the colors you use in your marketing materials. A good example is Coke and the color red. Have you ever wondered why Coke uses the color red in all of its marketing materials? It's because the color red is a major aspect of the company's branding theme.

2. Design and create a professional logo for your online business and use it in all your online communications and sales operations. Needless to say, your logo is a critical component of your brand's identification. Your logo is the symbol that represents who you are as a business or as a company. When customers see your logo, they are quickly reminded of your products, services, and what you stand for as a business.

With that said, it's important that you invest in a unique and high-quality business logo. Remember that your logo will be used in all materials that you use online. The logo should be a proper representation of your business and your products and services. If you don't have any background in logo design or graphics design, it's best that you outsource the creation of your logo. There are literally thousands of experienced and highly-skilled graphic designers out there who can create your logo for you.

3. Make use of a branded email signature.

You are an online business so majority of your communications with customers, business partners, and other concerned parties will be through email. You will probably be sending dozens if not hundreds of emails every single day depending on the size of your business. In short, your email signature is a powerful branding tool. You can add in your signature the name of your business, your logo, contact details, an RSS feed, or even links to your various social media pages. There are apps and tools like Wisestamp that can make the job easier for you. Using the tools allow you to create and customize great email signatures.

4. Use social media as a leverage.

Social media sites are probably the most powerful online branding tools today. According to recent statistics from the Pew Research Center, more than 75% of adults use social networking sites. That's huge. It means that if you want to reach as many people as possible with your branding message, you need to be on social media. You need to be on the biggest players in the social media scene like Facebook, Twitter, Instagram, LinkedIn, Pinterest, and YouTube. All of these social sites are free to use so there's no reason why you shouldn't sign up with them. You have very little to lose in using them to advance your branding goals.

5. Come up with an interesting and catchy slogan or tagline.

Just like your business logo, your slogan will be used in nearly all of your communication and marketing materials. Your slogan should be unique, short, straight to the point, and memorable. Furthermore, it should reflect the identity and brand of your business. Here's a quick rundown of some of the most well-known slogans and the businesses behind such slogans. Use these slogans as an inspiration in coming up with your own.

I'm lovin' it. – McDonalds
Just do it. – Nike
Have a break, have a Kit Kat – Kit Kat
Taste the rainbow. – Skittles
Eat fresh. – Subway
Don't be evil. – Google
Think different. – Apple
Impossible is nothing. – Adidas
The king of beers. – Budweiser

6. Add credibility to your brand by publishing testimonials in your websites and social media pages.

Testimonials are formal statements from customers, business partners, and other concerned parties that testify about the quality of your products and services. A testimonial can come from anywhere. It could be from a review written by a blogger. It could be from a review posted on a social site like Facebook. It could be from a letter sent to you via email. Testimonials are very powerful boosters for your business especially if you get a few from well-known names in your niche. For example, if you are selling a bicycle spare part and you get a testimonial from Lance Armstrong, your sales will surely hit the roof.

7. Start a blog.
This is one of the smartest things you can do for your business. Starting a blog is very easy. You can set up one in just a few minutes. You can host the blog inside your main website or you can get a separate domain for it. You also have the choice of using free blogging platforms like Wordpress, Tumblr, and Blogspot. As you can see, there are very little barriers to creating a blog. However, building a readership for your blog can be difficult. But if you consistently publish great content, your blog should grow a lot faster. The general role in blogging is that you should focus on topics that relate to your products and services. It's absolutely okay to go out of topic every once in a while but you shouldn't overdo it because going out of topic is one of the biggest reasons why readers lose interest in a blog.

8. Give your brand a face.
What does this mean? It literally means what it says. You should show your face as the owner and manager

of the business. If you run the business with several people, you can also consider showing their faces. The best way to do this is to put photos of yourselves in the bio sections or about pages in your websites. Consumers tend to trust businesses that aren't afraid to show the faces of their owners. Invest in professional photos. If your not comfortable being the face of the brand, hire talent.

9. Develop a customer reward plan.
Building a brand isn't just about attracting new customers, it's also about making sure that your current customers continue supporting your business down the line. One of the best ways to nurture customer loyalty is by giving them rewards. There are so many ways on how you can reward customers for their loyalty and patronage. You can offer discounts for customers who reach a certain purchase threshold. You can offer freebies. You can come up with membership programs wherein members have access to promos and discounts that non-members don't have access to.

10. Advertise your business.
Advertising is deeply enmeshed with branding. You have to be engaged in it if you really want to get the word out about your business. Advertising is a necessity especially if you are just starting out which means only a few people know about your products and services. Creating targeted ads will attract your initial waves of customers. The great thing about online advertising is that it's really affordable. It's not as expensive as advertising in traditional media outlets like newspapers, magazines, and television

programs. With a small and limited budget, you still have the potential to reach thousands if not millions of target customers.

These strategies aren't that difficult to implement. They take time to generate results, that's for sure. But as we have mentioned earlier, branding doesn't happen overnight. Patience is the key to success here. Think of Coca-Cola and their branding strategies. They've been doing it from the first day the company was set up. Several decades later, they are still following these branding strategies. That's patience. That's consistency. The same principles can be applied to branding an internet marketing business no matter how small or big it is.

Chapter 3:
How to Write a Comprehensive and Realistic Internet Business Plan

Don't start an internet business if you don't have a business plan. Ask any expert for advice and this is what they would tell you. Building a business without a plan is a recipe for failure. Don't get too overconfident about your business idea and products. If you want to start right, you should sit down first and write down your business plan. We are talking about small to medium-sized businesses here so all you need are the basic sections of a business plan. You can even write a concrete business plan in a few hours depending on the size of your business idea and the range of products you intend on selling.

Here's a quick overview of the most basic elements of a business plan:

1. Executive Summary

This is a concise overview of your business plan. It must be well-written, clear, and straight to the point. A person reading the executive summary should be able to get a clear understanding of what your business is about and what you intend to accomplish with it. The executive summary should contain your business name and location, a quick description of your products and services, your mission and vision statements, and the specific purpose of the plan. Most entrepreneurs would suggest that you write the executive summary last so that you can include important information from the other sections of the business plan.

2. Business or Company Description
If you are proposing the business idea to a potential partner or someone who can help you with funding, this is usually the section that read first because it's where their interests lie. With that said, you should make sure that this section is written properly and completely. The contents of this section may include the following:
- A quick summary of your short-term and long-term business goals
- The legal structure of your business
- A summary of your company's projected growth including your market and financial highlights
- A summary of your products, services, suppliers, and target customers
- A brief description of your business model, the nature of your operations, and the needs and demands of your business with regard supply.

3. Product and Service Description
Clearly describe the products you are selling or the services that you are offering. This doesn't have to be very detailed. Just make sure that a person reading the section can clearly determine what you are offering and the value you are providing. You should also include in this section some information about suppliers, manufacturers, costs, and estimated revenue you can generate from your sales. If possible, you should consider including high-quality photos of the line of products you are selling. This is very

important if you are going to present the business plan to a potential business partner or fund provider.

4. Market Analysis

This is where you provide realistic data about your target market, your competition, and the state of the market you want to penetrate. The contents of this section should come from a thorough market research that you have completed previously. You don't have to put all your findings here. Just create a summary of your findings. You can put the raw data in the appendix section. Your market analysis should include an evaluation of the strengths and weaknesses of your competition, a sketch of your targeted customer segments, a description of the current outlook in your niche, and projected marketing data for your services and products.

5. Organization and Management Team

This is where you create an outline of your company's organizational structure. That basically means identifying the owners, the partners, the management team, and the board of directors if there's any. You should come up with a simple organizational chart with descriptions of your key employees and business departments. Put yourself in the shoes of a potential employee or management team member. If you are looking at the organizational chart, you should be able to easily identify where you are in it and what your roles and responsibilities are.

6. Sales and Marketing Strategies

This is one of the most important sections of your business plan because the success of your proposed business will greatly depend on what you've written in this section. You need to offer a comprehensive description of your marketing and sales strategy. How do you intend to drive and increase sales? What are the online platforms you are going to use in your marketing campaigns? Which of these platforms will receive priority from you? Who are the people who will be responsible for implementing your sales and marketing strategies. These are some of the questions you have to answer in this section of the business plan.

7. Funding Requirements

In this section, you provide information how you are going to fund your business operations. Where are you getting the money? What's your funding model? Who are your potential credit providers? How are you going to repay these funds? These are the questions you are going to answer in this section of the business plan. You should include information for a worst-case scenario or a best-case scenario. There should be a plan A and a plan B for your funding requirements. If your funding dries up, there should be options for you on where you are going to seek more funding.

8. Financial Projections

This section of the business plan can be very complicated and technical. With that said, you are going to need the services of an accountant. You should only come up with your financial projections after you have completed your market research and analysis. Additionally, you should have already set goals for your business. Your financial projections will depend on these things. An accountant can't make financial projections of he doesn't understand your goals or the current state of your target market.

9. Appendix

Although this is an important part of the business plan, you have the option to include it or remove it from the main body of the business plan. Why? Because the appendix contains some confidential and proprietary information that shouldn't be viewed by anyone. With that said, you can decide to provide the appendix for a reader on an as-needed basis. For example, if a potential business partner wants to see detailed data about how you conducted your market research, then you can provide that person a copy of the appendix. Creditors or anyone who is helping you with the funding might ask for information that's contained in the appendix. Be ready to provide the information to them.

What you've read above is but a simplified version of an internet marketing business plan. These are just the basic sections of a business plan. You are free to add more sections as you deem necessary. You can also choose to break down each section into what's considered as sub-sections. The choice is yours. Be sure to spend some time here as it will give you the blueprint for your business. However don't get lost in the details.

Chapter 4:
How to Create Workable and Profitable Internet Marketing Campaigns

After setting up and launching your internet marketing business, the next obvious step is to start with your online campaigns with the ultimate goals of attracting visitors and converting them into paying customers. Of course, this is easier said than done. In the following guide, we are going to provide you with simple strategies and tips on how to create, run, and manage your internet marketing campaigns. Running an online campaign is going to cost you some money and if you don't get the results you wanted, then that basically means you are operating at a loss. With that said, you need to be serious about your online marketing campaigns.

When it comes to online campaigns, planning is everything. I'm assuming that you've completed your market research which means you only have to come up with marketing strategies on how to reach your identified target market. This is where you create a plan on how you are going to execute these strategies. Planning and proper execution. These are the main ingredients of a successful internet marketing campaign.

Choosing Your Marketing Channels
There are dozens of methods on how you can deliver your marketing message in front of your potential customers. Let's refer to these methods as marketing

channels. What you need to do is go over these channels and find the ones that you think are a good fit for your business and your business model. Which of these channels do you think have the ability to turn your audience from prospects into paying customers?

It can be tempting to try and use all of the channels you have access to. But trying everything at once will actually hurt your business instead of helping it. I would recommend that you choose three to five marketing channels and focus your efforts on them first. Using just a few selected channels makes sense because you can devote your time and resources on them. For example, you can choose to focus on search engine optimization, social media marketing, and advertising as your main marketing channels. Each of these channels has its own inherent complexities. In fact, using all three platforms will already have your hands full.

My point here is that you need to choose a few marketing channels and dedicate your time, focus, and resources on them. Don't ever make the mistake of assuming that the more platforms you use, the more effective your marketing campaign will be. This isn't the case at all. In fact, online entrepreneurs who devote their attention on a few platforms and channels tend to accomplish more than those who use too many channels.

Deciding on Your Marketing Budget
A common mistake among new online entrepreneurs is that they start marketing their products and services without taking into account first their

marketing budget. In most cases, they end up spending more than they can afford. To ensure that you don't go beyond your means, you should set up a realistic budget for your marketing campaigns. You should stick to that budget no matter what happens.

There's no standard procedure on calculating your marketing budget because it depends on a lot of factors like the size of your business, the type of products and services you are selling, the marketing channels you have chosen, and the niche you are trying to penetrate. For example, if you plan on advertising your products but you have a limited budget, you might consider advertising on social media sites instead of advertising through Google Ads. This is because advertising on social sites is usually a lot cheaper compared to the Google Ads program.

Try to give your budgets a specific time period. For example, you can set aside $200 a week for advertising on Facebook, $50 a day for advertising on Google Ads, or $1000 a month for direct advertising in blogs and websites that are relevant to your business. You need to be working with real numbers and specific budget estimates. It's okay if you get the amounts wrong during your initial marketing campaigns. It happens to most online marketers. You will get better in setting up budgets as you learn more about the industry and as you gain more experience.

Execution through the Marketing Channels You Have Chosen
After choosing your marketing channels and coming up with your budget, what's left to do is to execute

your marketing plan. This is where a lot of new online entrepreneurs stumble and fail. They may have a good plan and a well thought-out budget but they can't seem to pull the trigger to generate results. You see, executing a marketing plan isn't just about following the plan. It's also about adjusting your tactics if things aren't going as you expected. For example, you have chosen Facebook as a marketing channel. However, you soon realized that you aren't generating traffic or leads from the networking site as per your marketing projections.

So what should you do next? You pause your Facebook marketing efforts and spend some time to determine what is wrong. Why aren't you getting the results you want? Why are Facebook users not engaging with your marketing messages and ads? Find these problems and attempt to fix them. You also can't discount the possibility that maybe Facebook isn't just the right platform for the type of online business you have.

When promoting your business through different marketing channels, you should make it a point to follow the specific rules, policies, and guidelines that each channel requires from you. You are using platforms by third parties. If you do something that is against any of their rules and policies, you can get banned from the platform.

You should also take the time to track and measure the results you generate from each marketing channel. Tracking helps you determine which marketing channels are generating the most results for your business. For example, after tracking your marketing campaigns, you find out that social media marketing platforms capture internet leads more efficiently than other channels. This is a cue for you to ramp up your efforts in the social media sector of your campaigns.

Keep a record of all your results and measure them against the goals for each campaign. Include all of your spendings and actions. This will help you really zone in on what works and cut what doesn't.

Again, you need to be patient with your internet marketing campaigns. Take it slow and don't make decisions if you are not that sure about the results or if there are too many risks involved.

Chapter 5:
How to Use SEO to Fast-Track the Growth of Your Internet Business

Search engine optimization or SEO is something you should be knowledgeable about if you want to be a successful online entrepreneur. Always keep in mind the fact that majority of consumers who shop online usually start their search on Google. If you don't rank well on Google, there's a slim chance that your target customers will ever find out about your products and services. The only way for you to get to the top of the search results is through effective SEO.

In this chapter, we are going to discuss the most effective strategies that you can use to improve your rankings in Google and other search engines. Implementing SEO isn't as complicated nor technical as you might think. It can be frustrating at first but it gets much easier as you learn more about the process. Anyway, below are some tips on how you can optimize your website and make it rank better in the search results.

1. Make sure that your website is user-friendly.
This is the first thing that you should do. Review your website and make sure that it's running smoothly and loading quickly. Nothing turns off visitors faster than a website that takes forever to load. See to it that all your links are working properly. Broken links are a big no-no for search engines. Another aspect of your website that you should fine-tune is the navigation. A

visitor should be able to get from one page to another with ease. You should have simple and clear navigation tabs either at the top or on the side bar of your website.

2. Don't forget to perform comprehensive research about the keywords and phrases that you are going to use.

A lot of new online entrepreneurs often make the mistake of skipping this part. Keyword research and development is the foundation of your SEO strategy. You can't move forward with your optimization campaign if you don't have a list of keywords and phrases that you are going to target. All aspects of your optimization campaign will depend on these keywords. Whether you are doing content marketing or link building, you have to make use of your targeted keywords. If it's your first time to perform keyword research, we highly recommend that you use Google's own keyword planner. It's free to use. You can just sign in with your Gmail account.

3. Create sitemaps for your website.

This will help in making sure that search engines index the contents of your website. It's best that you create both XML and HTML versions of the sitemap. A sitemap allows the crawlers sent in by the search engines to reach all areas and sections of your website. A sitemap is especially necessary if you have a lot of archived content. There are sitemap generators that you can use to easily create sitemaps for your websites.

4. Make your site mobile-friendly.

You have to be aware of the fact that a huge number of people these days use their mobile phones to search about products and services online. If your website is not mobile-friendly, then you are missing out on a huge market. Having a mobile-friendly website is also a plus point for search engines like Google. The first step to make your website mobile-friendly is to make sure that it has a responsive design. If a person accesses the website through his phone, the design adjusts and adapts depending on the screen size of the mobile device.

5. Keep building authoritative backlinks for your website.

Your website will rank higher in the search results if readers perceive it as trustworthy and authoritative. And one of the best ways to build online authority and trust is through proper link building. If other websites are linking back to your website, this means that they are giving you votes on trustworthiness and credibility. Googe and other search engines look at these links and consider them when deciding how your website should rank in the search results. However, you should focus your backlinking efforts on attracting links from credible websites. Quality matters more than quantity. Getting one link from a credible website is better than getting ten links from ten spammy sites.

6. Install a SSL certificate on your website.

Online security is valued by Google especially these days wherein hackers are getting more blatant with their attacks. The point here is that Google will take into account the overall security of your website when determining how you should rank in the search results. Suffice it to say that if you have a secure website, you have better chances at ranking higher. With an SSL certificate, your website will be more secure for users and this boosts your site's credibility. Installing an SSL certificate is highly recommended especially if your site collects sensitive data (i.e. personal details, credit card numbers, passwords) from users.

7. Make use of SEO-friendly URLs.
Crawlers sent in by the search engines also look for clues in your URLs. The general rule is that it's better if you have descriptive URLs. They should be readable and they should contain keywords and phrases that are relevant to the contents of the page. For example, if the page is about social media marketing, it should contain the words social media and marketing.

8. Don't use Flash.
There's a reason why SEO experts always advise website owners to not use Flash in their websites. Of course, you can use Flash if it's absolutely necessary but you should tone down your usage of it. Flash is bad for SEO, it's that simple. Not only will Flash significantly slow down the loading speed of the website, crawlers also find it very difficult to index content and pages that contain Flash. Last but not the least; don't use Flash because it has a long history of security flaws, bugs, and malware. As we have discussed earlier, less secure websites are red flags for search engines.

9. Maintain a constant flow of high-quality content.

When it comes to content marketing, consistency is key. This is especially true if you are running a blog or a website that's similar to a blog. The more valuable content you churn out, the more visitors you attract. Mix up the type of content you produce. Don't just focus on creating articles, you should also create photos, videos, and infographics to make your website more appealing to various readers.

10. Connect your website with your social media pages.

Search engines now take into account social media chatter when ranking websites. If a website gets a lot of mentions and discussions in social sites like Facebook or Twitter, it is considered as more credible. These social media signs provide the website with more reasons to rank better in the search results.

If implemented properly and regularly, these practical SEO strategies can get your website closer to your ranking goals. If you attract more visitors from organic searches, you can close more sales. The growth of your business will be faster if you are getting a large chunk of your web traffic from search engines like Google and Bing.

Chapter 6:
Practical Tips for Generating Massive Traffic Towards Your Business Website

Traffic generation is not rocket science. It may take some time to master all the tricks but you will get there. Driving traffic to your website is something that you should take seriously. You should spend several hours every day on traffic generation especially if your internet business has just launched. You can make more money online if you master the art of attracting high-quality traffic. To help you get started, here's a rundown of the most effective methods you should be using.

1. Optimize your website for the search engines (i.e. Google, Bing).

I've discussed SEO in Chapter 5 so you should definitely go over that chapter again. SEO is very powerful in letting people know that your business and your products exist. Truth be told, SEO is the foundation of search marketing. Not only is it a way of attracting traffic, it's also a way to make sure that you remain competitive. If your competitors are better in optimizing their websites, then you will be losing out your customers to them.

2. Try email marketing.

Almost everyone who uses the internet has an email address. This is because you can't use a lot of online services if you don't have an email address. In order to market effectively via email, you should set up a newsletter so that you can start building your email list. People who subscribe to your newsletter are automatically added to your list. Through the newsletter, you update your subscribers about the latest developments in your business (i.e. new product announcements). Attract subscribers through lead marketing. Essentially, you can set up websites with free offers in exchange for an email address.

3. Set up a blog for your business website.
You can either build a blog inside your main website or you can set up a separate domain for it. A blog is a great platform for creating extra content for both loyal customers and potential customers. It also happens that blogs are loved by search engines which means they rank really well in the search results. If you are consistently updating it then your going to rank really well for your search terms.

4. Engage with your customers online.
Don't forget to interact with your customers. If they send you emails, make it a point to answer them. If they leave comments in your website or in your blog, respond whenever you can. The goal here is to let your customers know that you genuinely care about their concerns. Don't just be all about posting and never interacting. Effective internet marketing is a two way conversation between you and your customers.

5. Use the Analytics tool to understand how visitors are interacting with your website.
There's a lot of reasons why you should use the Google Analytics tool. First of all, it's free so you have nothing to lose in taking advantage of it. But the most

important reason why you should use it is that it provides you with valuable insights about your website visitors. You can learn about where your visitors are coming from, which links they are clicking, which sections of your website are getting the most attention, and which external websites are referring traffic to your website.

6. Write content for other websites as a guest writer.

This is called content marketing. You produce content with the goal of having these published in other websites. In return for the free content, the host website puts a link within the content or within the author bio that links back to your own website. Collaboration is an excellent way of building more interest in your brand whilst also making connections with experienced people who can even mentor and lift you up. Reach out to influencers in your field.

7. Create a landing page.

This is a great strategy if you are selling products. You create landing pages for the products. You optimize these landing pages to attract visitors from search engines and other sources like social media sites. When a visitor gets to the landing page, you have them redirected to your main website. For this reason, most online marketers utilize several landing pages depending on the number of products or services they are selling.

8. Be active in social media.

Chances are most of your target customers are using social networks like Facebook, Twitter, Instagram,

YouTube, etc. You should take the time to engage with your customers through these sites. Social media enables you to connect with your target audience in a more open and personal manner. This build trust and loyalty over time.

9. Advertise your business and products on social media.

Engaging with people on social media is great but if you want to double or triple your social media reach, you should consider buying ads in the platforms you are using. The good news is that the biggest social media platforms today like Facebook, Twitter, and Instagram have their own advertising programs. Through these advertising programs, you can boost the reach of our posts, updates, and tweets. Advertising on social media these days can be incredibly rewarding since you are able to zone in on specifics such as location, age and interest. Utilize your market research to build effective advertising campaigns.

10. Advertise online using Google Ads.

Google has the best advertising program online. So if you want to advertise your website, you should definitely use their program. It's very affordable as well and you have complete control over your budget. You don't have to pay more than you can afford. You can make use of Google Keywords tool to identify the best keywords to implement.

11. Submit your content to aggregator sites.

A content aggregator is a type of social networking site that collects and curates content from all over the web. Content in these sites are user-generated which means anyone can register and submit content. Great examples of aggregator websites include Reddit, Feedly, Panda, Techmeme, Metacritic, and PopUrls.

12. Give out freebies.
Everybody loves free items. It doesn't matter if it's a free ebook, a free shirt, or a free gift voucher. People will be lining up to get their hands on them. Use the free item as a front to entice people to visit your website. You can promote the giveaway outside of your website but for people to be eligible to receive it, they need to visit your website first.

13. Run online contests.
This is one of the most powerful ways on how to build hype for your business. A successful contest can attract thousands of new visitors to your website. To promote your online contests, you should use as leverage several marketing channels like social media and paid advertising.

14. Create free online courses then use these as leverage to attract more people.
You can offer your knowledge and expertise for free in the guise of online courses. People who like your courses will likely search for more content from you by visiting your website. It's all about building trust and adding value. If they like what you do and become a fan of yours than that is likely to lead to revenue for your business.

I am not in any way suggesting that you should use every single one of these methods. How many of these methods you are going to implement will depend on the amount of time you have in your hands. What I would suggest is that you find the methods that generate the best results for your website. Experiment and then ramp up your efforts on these specific methods to scale the results.

Chapter 7:
How to Convert Website Visitors into Paying Customers

Enticing people to visit your website is just the first step in online sales. Driving traffic is important but you should also learn how to convert your visitors into paying customers. This is a lot more difficult to do because you don't have control over the spending capabilities of your visitors. However, there are things you can do to increase the chances that a visitor buys something from you.

Keep the Navigation Simple

Don't you find it frustrating when you visit a shopping website and you can't seem to get around as quickly as you would like? The site navigation is so undefined that you waste a lot of time trying to find which tabs you should click. This is a serious problem that can scare away a lot of potential buyers. You should review your website and make sure that the navigation system is as smooth and clear as possible.

Highlight Your Products and Services

This is obviously a no-brainer but a lot of new online entrepreneurs tend to take it for granted. You should use a website design that prominently displays your offers. Think of your website as the front facade of a physical store. Your best products should be prominently displayed front and center. Implementing this simple rule can quickly increase your conversion rate especially if you receive a lot of your traffic from search engines.

Make Use of Customer Testimonials

You can improve your conversion rate by simply featuring customer testimonials in your website. As much as possible, you should only use independent and verifiable testimonials. For example, if a blogger posted a good review of product or service in his blog, you can use quotes from the review as testimonials for your products. You can also use reviews and comments left by your customers in your social media pages. The main point in publishing testimonials is to provide your potential clients of the potential value that they can get from your product/service.

Offer Lots of Freebies

When you offer a freebie, most consumers would look at it as a bonus. Research studies show that when a product is tied up with a bonus, the likelihood that the customer purchases the product can increase by up to two-fold. To make the freebie even more difficult to turn down, you can provide a limited time period for the freebie. For example, the freebie can only be available to customers who buy it from January 1 to January 30. The limited timeframe makes the customer feel like he might miss out should he decide not to buy the item right now.

Make Sure That the Visitor Understands the Value of Your Offers

For every product or service that you list in your website, you should provide a detailed description of it. The aim is to inform the customer about the product's value and how it can help him. This is where your sales pitch skills come into play. Don't just say "buy this" or "buy that", you should provide reasons why the customer should buy the product. What are its features? What can the products do? How long will the product last? What are other customers saying about the product? Does it come with a guarantee or a warranty? These are just some of the things that customers would like to know. And you need to provide them with clear and straightforward answers.

As you implement the strategies above, I would recommend that you track and keep a log of your progress. Building a website isn't always a one task job. A lot of the time it's all about refinement to create the best version. Of course that changes over time as well so you need to stay relevant. It's important that you identify the methods that are improving your conversion rates so that you can focus more of your attention on them.

Chapter 8:
How to Drive Consistent Sales through Email Marketing

Email marketing is among the oldest online marketing strategies. There's a reason why it has lasted so long and remains as relevant today as it was twenty years ago. It works. It increases sales. It improves conversion rates. It's as simple as that. If you want to maintain your customer base, email marketing is a great way to achieve it. In this chapter, we are going to look into some of the things you can do to generate more results from email marketing.

1. Utilize personalization to improve customer retention.

Email personalization involves creating messages that cater to the needs and wants of the recipients. If you have customers from various demographics, you should customize your messages to cater to each demographic. Make sure that your email copy reads like it was written for a human. A common mistake among new email marketers is that they make use of generic messages that they then send in bulk to all their customers no matter how segmented these customers are. This strategy is like shooting a shotgun into the dark hoping that a shrapnel will find its mark. It doesn't make any sense at all. So what you need to do is personalize your messages based on the sectors, segments, or types of recipients you are sending them to.

2. Take the time to craft catchy and interesting subject lines.

When you receive a message in your inbox, the first thing you read is the subject line, right? If the subject line doesn't interest you, you either mark the message as "read" even though you didn't actually read it or you send it straight to the trash file. You don't want this to happen to the messages that you send to your email list. The subject line is so important that some marketers spend more time writing and rewriting it than writing the message itself. Make people curious and interested to open your emails.

3. Add dynamic content to your messages.
Simply put, dynamic content is HTML plated within the message that changes and adapts based on the end user or recipient. Dynamic content plays a very important role in increasing user engagement. There are dozens of dynamic content tools that you can use to make the process easier. Such tools include Act-On, Avari, Bluecore, Boomtrain, Cordial, Kickdynamic, LiveIntent, and Movable Ink. Most of these tools charge for their services but the expense is trivial compared to the additional sales that you can generate because of them.

4. Track recipient behavior with analytics.
Install tracking snippets in your email campaigns so that you can see how your recipients are interacting with your messages. With tracking, you can learn which links are being clicked, which sections of the message are getting the most attention, and which segments of recipients have the highest engagement rates. With the data you gather through tracking, you can further improve your email campaigns in order to generate better results in the next campaigns.

5. Implement A/B testing in your email campaigns.

A/B testing refers to the marketing practice of using two different email ad copies with the intention of tracking them and learning which ad copy generates better results. For example, you can use images in the first copy and use no images in the second copy. You send the ad copies to the same numbers of recipients. You then measure how recipients interact with the ad copies. At the end of the campaign, you should be able to identify which copy generated better engagement and better results.

6. Invest in automated email

Many if not all of the above tasks can be automated and there are specific email programs to take care of that. When someone enters their email the automation takes care of everything. It will send them a chain of emails over time that you set up once. You can then track the results in the program and fine tune as you go. Check out Aweber, Mailchimp or Mailerlite.

As you may have realized by now, email marketing can be a time-consuming endeavour. You must be willing to invest a lot of your time and resources into your email campaigns. The time investment may be huge but the rewards can be huge as well if you do things properly. In fact, email marketing is so effective for a lot of online entrepreneurs that they generate most of their sales from their email campaigns. The point here is that email marketing can be a significant source of sales for your internet business.

Conclusion:
Now Is the Time to Take Action

If you've read this book in its entirety, then you are more than prepared to get your online business to the next level. With the strategies, tips, and advice I have provided in this book, you can build and grow a six-figure business.

That's not an exaggeration. You can definitely earn thousands of dollars every week from your business if you play your cards right. It's going to be a slow start but if you apply what we have discussed here, you can increase your numbers, improve your sales, ramp up your conversions, and earn serious money.

However, these things will only happen if you take action. All the strategies I have discussed in this book mean nothing if you don't apply them. As the saying goes, action speaks louder than words. Go over the chapters again if you have to. Just make sure to implement the strategies the way we have tackled them in this book.

Last but not the least, I would like to thank you for availing and reading this book. It means a lot to me. I hope that you found here the type of value that you were looking for. And I need one last favor from you. If you know of someone who might also be interested in reading this book, feel free to recommend this book to him or her. Thank you and good luck with your online business.

You can keep up to date with the latest information and resources from me at my website.

https://wswainbrand.com/

Addictive Content Marketing: *Drive Demand, Maximize Traffic, Sales, and Brand Recognition*

William Swain

Contents

Introduction

Content marketing is a powerful strategy that no matter what business or industry you are in will time and time again produce serious results. It is the strategy of creating and then distributing valuable information to a selected target market with the ultimate goal of profit driven customer actions. In respect of this definition whatever you consider creating for your market can be defined as content marketing. For example this might include blogs, articles, white papers, video, infographics, podcasts, webinars and so on.

Now you may be thinking "I've been there, tried that and it's not for me." Or maybe you're curious about the subject of content marketing but are not really sure where to get started. Regardless, I can guarantee you that it will work to grow your business and it doesn't have to be complicated. You just have to know what to focus your efforts onto.

Content marketing starts with the user in mind

Back in the old days customers relied on salesmen to help them with choosing the best products or services. Salesmen would listen to and interpret what the customer was saying into an offer or a solution. Nowadays salesmen have in most situations been replaced with online shopping, social media and online review sites. But this is good news because we now have full access to huge data collection agencies working twenty four seven providing you with useful information. Plus for the most part they are completely free.

The challenge today is creating something that's worth sharing and that people will love. In essence to create something new and pivotal. Or something of great quality and value to the audience. Then you have more chance of higher traffic and social shares.

Focus on quality over quantity

Anyone can create content but creating quality content that keeps your audience engaged is a whole different story. Your customers and clients are more selective than ever before in deciding where and who to devote their time and attention to. But if you're committed to growing your business in the long run then you know content marketing is the key.

Before you create any kind of content get conscious of your marketing goals or what it is that you're aiming to accomplish. This is what will determine and streamline your message in turn giving all pieces of content a strategic purpose. For example if you're looking to generate leads you'll want to brainstorm content that provides a quick win and entices visitors to hand over their email address. Or if your goal is to increase sales and you're working further down the funnel then you may want to consider a webinar that showcases your products and services.

Every piece of content should bring prospects one step closer to becoming your loyal customers. But if your brand-new and you've got no existing following it doesn't matter how good your content is, because no one will see it. People who've already built an email list up and who have a large social media following will always get way more exposure. Therefore your success relies heavily on having an audience.

Remember that no one is born with an audience. Spend some time going through the origin stories of well-known people in your industry and you will always hear a variation of the same story. There will be this slow burning process, a dedication to their craft and of really being a nobody for a period of time. Where they're putting in a lot of effort to produce good content. Maybe they get one extra well-known guest on their podcast which leads to another, then leads to another and snowballs. Or maybe they published a post that got a lot of shares on Facebook which then introduces them to a popular podcaster. Then they get an interview on the podcast which moves on to them to guest speaking at an event and getting invitations, or to write a book and so on. All these little doors open up to bigger and bigger doors.

Trends are moving more and more towards who is the most creative or who's got the most reach in terms of what they've already established or the influencers they know. If you can't compete with that or if your content doesn't resonate with your audience you're going to be left in the cold. Build a brand that people want to follow and engage with. Branding is more important than ever that. As a brand you've got to have a more compelling story and higher production quality to cut through.

Your audience want to feel seen, heard and acknowledged. An easy way to do that is to make sure you're putting them in the spotlight. The spotlight can either be on you or your audience. If the spotlights on you the focus of your word is likely on your passion, cleverness and your goals. However when you shift that spotlight over to your audience the focus of your words is on them. Now unfortunately most of us get this wrong especially when it comes to our writing. Most of the time we all shine way too much of that spotlight on ourselves and not enough of it onto our customers.

When your target market finds your content and consumes it they feel like they're starting to develop a relationship with you. This will help to position you as an expert in your field who offers helpful and valuable information. Naturally this encourages them to know, like and trust you which is ultimately the precursor to them becoming a lead.

Bottom line is it's useless to create content your target market doesn't care about. It really defeats the purpose of content marketing altogether. This is why every single piece of content you create should hinge on knowing and understanding your audience.

Let's look at how we can achieve that.

Start With Your Audience In Mind

Before you create any content you need to get clear on who your target audience is. Research the type of content that resonates with them and how they prefer to consume it. Creating all of your content on that foundation with purpose will save you time and guarantee that you hit your targets.

People are bombarded by tons of messages each day. Reports average that to be over two thousand messages per day. Yet we can only recognize about fifty of them. Then out of those fifty you're only going to remember about four. Naturally that will come from the content that connects with us. Thinking with the customer in mind will give you a sense for what topics and issues will impact their lives. You can then leverage content to deepen your connection with them. The more they feel understood the easier it gets for them to know like and trust you. Understanding how your audience consumes information is a really critical way of shaping your content strategy.

Creating an ideal customer avatar will ensure you are creating the right content. Your avatar should include information such as interests, age, profession and geographic location. Think about where your customers are, and how can you deliver value through a strong content marketing strategy.

Identify where your customers are spending their time online:
- Are they on Facebook?
- Instagram?
- Medium?
- YouTube?

- Blogs?

Identify your customers:
- Interests
- Age
- Profession
- Location

Consider those points and then identify how their life will be happier, brighter or more productive with your content. If you haven't figured out some big problems or benefits of your potential audience then that's a great place to start.

The other great place to start is user experience level. When you create content you want to make sure that it is targeting a specific experience level. Maybe that's someone who's been in your niche or industry for less than a year. Before you ever write a single piece of content it's important that you identify the information gap. That is going to be different based on whether someone's a beginner, intermediate or really advanced. For example if you sell advertising, you could target complete beginners who know nothing about Google AdWords. Or you could target intermediate people who've maybe tried AdWords on their own and haven't gotten the results that they're looking for and so they start looking for answers to questions. All of a sudden your content pops up and meets them where they are.

That's a great example of combining the user experience level and the questions they need to buy. Then as you produce that content you speak right to the ideal customer wherever they are in their experience continuum. After you've identified that experience level make sure that you look at what are the questions that they need answered.

Market Research Tools

Google Trends
One of the most valuable and least utilized tools available for determining current trends in the marketplace is Google Trends. In a nutshell it tracks and provides topics that are becoming more and more popular. It can even provide those topics by regions. This is an indispensable tool that offers massive value but is not used on mass. Therefore by using it you are privileged to valuable insights that your competitors are likely to not be aware of.

Google Keyword Tool & Google Alerts
Another great way to discover what customers are thinking is to utilize the Google keyword tool. Type in a keyword or phrase and it will display the number of searches for it and also an auto populate list of suggested keywords that people are looking for every month. Combine those with the use of Google Alerts which allows you to monitor what's happening with your customers right now. Enter a keyword that you want to track into the search bar at the top of the page and then Google will email you whenever this keyword appears online. You can use this to track your business name, the industry you're in, your own name, your competitors and pretty much anything else you can think of.

Facebook Insights & Twitter Audiences
Facebook insights is another great market research tool to discover the content which resonates best with your specific market. Now of course in order to use this you will require a Facebook business page which is a valuable asset to have. You can then use it to analyze which posts are the most

engaging. From there you can decide on the best fit for content that your target market will be the most interested in.

Twitter can also be used to analyze posts that are the most engaging. Again as with Facebook you can utilize this to test out various types of content and see which create the most engagement. In addition Twitter also has a much underutilized but powerful tool named audiences which offers the ability for you to focus in on the topics and content that your target market are most interested in.

Using any one of these tools can help you gain a better understanding of your customers. In turn this will help you create a clear and compelling picture of your customers wants, needs and behaviors. Thus allowing you to better understand them and to come up with value providing services and solutions to their problems.

Build Your Library

There are four pillars of content, written, audio, image and video. The first step you need to take is to figure out which type of content to produce. Some people love watching videos and spend hours a day on YouTube. Whilst some people spend hours a day listening to podcasts or reading blog posts. Successful content marketing requires that your really good at using the platform that your ideal audience is already engaging with it. Decide on the medium that your most comfortable with and then determine which your target market enjoys the most. Then that is going to be a match made in heaven. Don't be afraid to experiment and adapt.

Research & Collect Content

Build out an idea library and it will save you a ton of time. There are many different ways to build up your library and there a lot of many types of content inside of the four pillars. Consider the different types. With written content, one type could be customer reviews. You can capture all these customer reviews and build out a stock pile of these reviews that you can trickle out on social media over time, or on all of your different content sources and platforms. Another example could be infographics or stats. Do you have specific infographics or stats for your industry? These don't necessarily have to be graphics and stats that you've created. They could be created by other sources. Other examples could be finding quotes, such as industry specific quotes or quotes that you have come up with yourself.

Consider the different types of videos. Those could be vlogs of your travels, life and so on. Or maybe you make engaging or instructional videos with a funny twist. For images, you could use photos of your company or of your products and so on. Then with audio you could create voice notes, podcasts and so on. Regarding audio content you can create podcasts, audiobooks, short clips and much more.

Coming Up With Ideas

Ask most marketers and they'll tell you the big challenge is not in creating content but rather in always being able to come up with content ideas. So if it seems like your time and energy are spent brainstorming ideas rather than really creating content then you're not alone.

Sometimes ideas might come at the most random times. Keep a record of those ideas as they come to you. Evernote is a great way to store and organize your ideas in notes. It is both web and mobile friendly and that's just one of the many options available to start keeping an idea bank that you can refer back to. If all else fails a pen and piece of paper can work pretty well too. Here are some other ways to come up with more content ideas.

Google
The first place you can start with is Google. Type in your search term or niche into Google and it will automatically tell you the most common relevant things that people are looking for. Copy those down into an idea generation note file. You'll also notice that the search will autocomplete phrases. This is automatically giving you more ideas of what people are looking for. In addition if you go down to the bottom you will notice there are even more search ideas for you to use.

Find the topics that other leaders in your niche are writing about. Then you can research those and understand what they are about. You can do then keyword research on those to see if they acquire high search volumes. If it's something you like, know about and is interesting for your audience then you can go in and create content on that subject matter.

YouTube

YouTube is another huge search engine full of content. Search for terms relevant to your subject matter. Take note of what the top ten to twenty different videos are about. Look at suggested videos or other related videos in the niche. Take note of the production quality, presentation style, editing and SEO of the video title, description and metrics. Apply these to your content with your own twist.

Quora

A question-and-answer website where people from all around the world are able to ask questions. Then people from all around the world can answer those questions. Type in your term into the search bar and results will display of actual questions posed by real people. There is even a more button at the bottom which auto populates more relevant results. This is a great resource for your content marketing since those are essentially people from your target market.

Yahoo Answers

Another one similar question and answer site is Yahoo Answers. It's essentially the same kind of website as Quora where people ask questions and have them answered by registered users. Again another powerful resource for content marketing research and idea generation.

Niche Forums

Niche forums are absolutely fantastic places to get ideas for content marketing To find them simply search your term + forum into Google and it will come up with relevant forums. Visit those forums and look at the relevant threads. Focus on how many different replies there are. On the majority forums you can sort by number of replies. This is how you can identify what the most engaging and most commented on topics are. You then have the ability to go kind of be a fly on the wall in these conversations. That will give you a lot of really powerful ideas that you know are engaging to the target audience.

In addition you should also be engaging inside of these forums. Avoid promoting your content but instead focus on engaging and adding value in the forums. Answer questions, pose topics and so on. Create an account with a link to your website in your forum signature then people can check out more about you if they like what you post.

Amazon

Search for books within your niche. Identify the most popular ones, then click into the book and look inside. This allows you to see the table of contents. Essentially these are all of the ideas that this author thought were the most important content to communicate to someone who bought the book. I'm obviously not advocating that you go plagiarize or steal their ideas. Instead I'm trying to give you idea synthesis, generation and inspiration.

Answer The Public

This is a great tool to find more content ideas. Visit the website and just type in the topic that you're interested in finding out content ideas on. It will then load lots of different questions that people happen to be asking about that subject.

There's so many different ideas you could come up with for content. It will even compare different subjects for you. You can then download all the results as a CSV or an Excel spreadsheet.

Syndicating Content

Focus on creating that one piece of great content that can be syndicated into more pieces. Then you can get more work done in less time and effort. Maybe you get that one great idea for some content. What you can do is to syndicate and repurpose that content. Say you invest some time into writing an exceptional blog post. Syndicate that into three or four bite-sized scripts or videos. Or maybe you did an interview, use the show notes as standalone blog posts from slides to social media posts, tweetable tips to infographics and much more. One well-thought-out piece of content can be converted into just about any marketing medium. This will eliminate having to create lots of brand new ideas.

Let's say your making a corporate video. That would include a bunch of different subjects. You might talk about your culture, your history, services and so on. Most companies don't have just one service or one product. You might highlight a customer story a testimonial and then a call to action. This is kind of the general flow of what a corporate video might look like.

Try to make this content last and stretch it into even more videos or posts. From that one video you could break it down into an extended spot talking about company culture. Then you could do an extended a video about the company history. How you started as a company, the humble beginnings, things you've learned along the ways and so on. Then there could be a service overview which is really talking about the features, benefits and values you have as an organization. If you have sub services talk about those too. So for example if you offer real estate services, a sub service would be supporting buyers or taking care of the loan documents and so on. Add to that you could have a number of different testimonial videos from customers.

All of these videos compiled together make your three to five minute corporate video. Split up into all these smaller videos, posts or audio you could post fresh content every month for as long as you want.

Another example of syndicating content could be from an e-book. For example you might be writing about wood craft. This could include an introduction to woodcraft. The terminology of woodcraft. The history of woodcraft, how it is used today and how it was used in the past. Maybe there are new trends or new ways of working with woodcraft or even some of the most well known people in the industry. You could even turn all of these topics into individual books, blog posts videos and more. Then as you please you can compile them or present them in different bundled ways and so on.

Following on you can distribute all of the supporting content leading up to your primary content which is the big ebook. Launch the fact that you have an e-book onto your website. Take one of the smaller ebooks and advertise that in order to get this free ebook give us your email address and we'll send it off to you. Then once a week after or maybe once a month release a blog post covering a different section of the e-book and at the very bottom link to the whole ebook you can buy.

Best Practices

The best practice for building a content library is to keep it simple. You can always just use your phone to create content. There are so many famous content marketers who do that and it does very well for them. Keeping things simple results in your content being easier to consume and also requires a lot less time invested in the creation. Focus on being clear, concise and easy for your audiences to understand. If you are a novice then go with the topics you are well versed in so that you avoid wasting time in researching. Then you are more likely to captivate and hold the attention of your audience with focused uncomplicated information.

Whilst keeping it simple try to choose longer and less frequent content over shorter and more frequent content. There are obviously massive exceptions to this rule but the takeaway point is that social media and search engines tend to prefer longer form content because usually it provides more value to the audience. So make producing this longer form type of content your number one goal.

Next be sure that your content is relevant to the modern times. Google tends to rank newer content much higher up. Keep updating your old content and you will out rank people that are regurgitating the same old repurposed content. Audiences are tired of reading, "the twelve marketing strategies that will triple your profits" or "the top ten ketogenic exercises" and so on. Keep it fresh and valuable.

As you create and build up content over time you will be building a valuable and powerful asset of information, resources and material which you can mine and extract from in the future. Once you create content it's yours forever and it works around the clock to build your business.

People succeed because of what they do over time. Famous musicians have lots of albums. Famous actors have lots of movies. Famous authors have lots of books and so on. Every piece of content you produce is one step closer to a breakthrough.

How To Write Content

Writing and creating great content is part art and part science. The science part comes from researching. Then, selecting the right delivery method and finally understanding audiences well enough to know what type of content they will get the most value from. The art comes in combining all of these elements to create powerful and effective pieces of content that educate, inform or entertain.

Writing excellent and engaging content can often feel like a massive hurdle to overcome. However the results are often more than worthy of the required effort. Justification for the effort comes from knowing that whatever you distribute is going to help you to improve and build your business. Keeping your content on point is the number one valuable thing that you can do. Any potential customers who discovered your content did so because they wanted to find out more about the subject you marketed. It is your obligation to provide the right content to them. In order to achieve this your content must stay as relevant to the subject matter as possible.

All content should first be planned out in writing. Begin with a brainstorm. Take out a notebook and thought dump everything into it. Start forming sentences, paragraphs and write as many words as possible within a short timeframe. Forget what you learned in school about the rules of writing. Write your marketing materials in the style of which you would normally speak to people. This way it will connect with them more naturally. Make sure to keep the tone consistent. It's okay to break and bend a few grammar rules here and there. After all, grammatically correct text often makes speaking pretentious and harder to speak. If your readers have to check out a dictionary all the time then you are making them work way too hard. Technical terminology will likely make people bored and tired of reading. Writing beautiful content should be reserved for the Shakespeare's of our generation.

Storytelling

Insert a storytelling element, it doesn't have to be about you. It can be just something well-known or interesting and that's what makes it powerful. Review if an idea is good enough by checking that it has a beginning, middle and end. People will always want to know how did you make your first million dollars or how did you lose thirty pounds in the last six weeks. Or how did you get pregnant after trying for four years and so on. Even if you're not a superstar but maybe you've done something that's really inspiring or compelling. Well then there's a story that you have access to. That's how you create content that will stand out.

Think through your own back catalogue of ideas and situations you've lived through. Accomplishments, experiences or even any people you know. Weave things together into a narrative with a story arc that leads to a conclusion tailored to your audience. The only way that you could potentially succeed today is if you focus on creating powerful content that really resonates with people. Put in that extra effort or ideally have a unique story. If content is compelling then it will stand the test of time. Find those unique stories and over time you'll get those leverage pieces of content that deliver traffic long term. if you're shouting your name backed by a powerful story, people are more likely to listen.

Writing Tips

When your writing focus on small wins and keep your paragraphs shorter. Human minds are built to celebrate success. This is a big reason for the designers of video games adding in lots of small achievements to games. The feeling of being rewarded for your efforts creates addictive behaviours. Apply this to your content. With every short paragraph the reader should get a feeling of victory which drives them to the end.

Break the writing up into lists, bullets, or even highlight the most important parts and actions. In turn this will also give your readers reasons to come back to your content should they experience any similar issues later on down the road. By creating actionable content you're giving your audience things that they can try immediately. Incidentally this is another great way to influence more people to potentially subscribe to you or buy any of your products or services. In effect it builds a relationship of trust because you have provided tasks which they can test for themselves that will give them the experience of immediate results. Nothing sells better than positive results.

When it comes to editing, break it up into different phases. During the first phase read it out loud as if you're speaking to somebody. See where it gets too complicated or if it doesn't flow naturally. When reading most people do so aloud in their head which will make any breaks in the flow of text obvious. Again don't worry about it being grammatically correct.

Consider if you managed to cover all of the areas that you wanted to. Do you need to add more in some areas? Ensure the depth of content is of adequate length. Sometimes things can get fluffy and you may need to cut parts out. Less is more and this will optimize your writing with more purpose and strength. Finally make sure to review the spelling, grammar and flow.

Time Constraints

We tend to drag our feet when we know there's a lot of time to complete a project. If we have a week we'll take a week. But if we have a day that sense of urgency sharpens and motivates us to deliver before crunch time. You can apply the same result when producing content by setting a timer with the goal to finish before the time runs out. Not only does the force you to make progress at a steady pace it also lights up creative momentum that prevents you from losing your train of thought. Valuable gems can be created from applying a little bit of pressure.

If you are still struggling don't worry not all of us are born natural writers, and that is just fine. Instead you can always hire a professional writer under your direction. Writing services can be found for an affordable price and that will likely result in a higher quality piece of written content.

Headlines

If you want to generate more social shares for your content then it's all about the headline. To write amazing headlines you need to consider a few things. First of all make sure your headline is around five to seven words in length. When your headlines are too long for some reason it's just overwhelming and people don't want to share it. When it's too short people don't really know what your content is about.

Next thing to consider is using adjectives. When using words like "effortlessly" what will happen is people will be like "oh wow ten *effortlessly* ways to double my search traffic, that sounds way better than ten ways to double your search traffic". Adjectives paint pictures and sounds in people's minds. Create a mystery or an easy pathway. For example "the seven benefits of green tea". Or all those "get rich quick" titles. People respond well to intrigue and quick fix solutions.

Always remember that people have reasons for coming to your content. Make sure with that your headlines you deliver on any promises made because then you need to ensure your content provides the answers they are looking for. Try analyzing your content from a potential customers perspective and that will help you to know whether you've sufficiently answered in addition to coming up with any other questions they might have.

A/B test your headlines. Every thirty days or so change your headlines. Then if you get more traffic and clicks stick with it. In addition test on Twitter. Create four or five different variations of your headline and tweet them out. Then see what gets the most traffic to your website. Whatever gets the most traffic, you should use.

Add Images
According to Forbes, content with images gets over ninety percent more views than content without images. That's certainly worth considering. Images can turn an average post into something great. However using images just for the sake of it is wasteful unless it adds value to the reader. Look for, creative infographics which will make your content much more easy to read through and understand. At the end of the day you don't want to get to the end of an article with more questions. When you find images that evoke emotions your audience will be better able to relate to your content.

Creating Images

Make use of Canva which is both free and available to use online. It's really easy to use and you can get started with their templates. They have a whole lot of designers who create these amazing templates. For example say if you wanted to create a social media graphic for Instagram. Click on the template and it gives you the correct specifications and then it gives you a whole host of templates that are all free. You can then go in and change the background colors, text, images and so on.

People are bored of seeing the same old stock photographs. Go to Canva and create your own images. You don't need to be a professional designer. It's a really easy to use tool to use and it will bring you more traffic.

Focus On Quality

We all know that there is a lot of content being published all the time. Therefore we really want to make sure that we stand out and are producing enough quality content. Respect your audience's time and avoid wasting it with fluff pieces. Instead deliver the actual value and content that they're looking for. Content is really the only way that you're talking to someone consistently throughout the entire customer lifecycle. Traditionally a lot of marketers think of content as awareness and engagement focus but really content needs to follow the entire customer lifecycle all the way through.

An Effective Distribution Strategy

Benjamin Franklin once said "by failing to prepare you are preparing to fail". This rings true in almost every aspect of content marketing. Without drawing up a clear strategy to guide your content, you risk wasting time and effort on creating pieces that fail to connect with your target audience. Every battle is won before it's ever fought. People who understand the power of strategy realize that success is actually architected and planned out in advance. Those who invest the most time in strategic planning are usually ones who are the most successful. Even though planning often doesn't seem like it's doing much, yet it is so powerful. Every minute you spend in planning saves ten minutes in execution.

Content marketing is a two-part strategy. Step one is the creation and distribution is the second step. Both are necessary for a content marketing strategy to be effective. Once you have your content produced it's time to work on distributing it. You can achieve this through a number of channels such as email, social media, paid advertising, SEO and so on.

The most efficient and effective way to make content marketing work for you is to be laser focused on what produces results. A strong content marketing strategy is important to your brand because you want to be in front of people all the time, driving value. Remember a little planning goes a long way

Choose your promotion strategy.
- Are you going to be doing advertising?

- Are you going to be doing SEO?
- Are you going to reach it out to influencers?

These are just three quick examples of how you can promote your content. Because if you don't have a solid promotion strategy your content will not be visible. A lot of people have the old mentality of creating content and then just cranking it out. Well if you do only that then you're probably not going to get ranked very well on Google or social media. That might have worked before when content was somewhat of a novelty and it wasn't as difficult to break through. However today it is much more difficult to cut through the noise. Even month by month it seems to get harder to break through. Content is going up whilst engagement is going down. The economic value of content is zero unless people see it and share it. The amount of content is going up whilst the cost to stand out is also going going up. That cost can come from creating investing in better content or advertising spend.

Free Promotion
Spend more time promoting than writing. It doesn't matter how good of a content piece you write it's not going to be seen unless you promote it. There a number of great ways to promote which are free to do. Research all the other competing articles on the web. Click on the view shares button and it will show you every single person who shared those articles. Contact those people and send them your content. That simple trick will help you get more social traffic instantly since it is targeted at the right people.

Contribute in groups that you're posting in. Don't just spam your stuff in the group because you will frustrate the admin and you could get booted out from the group. Answer questions and engage with those audiences. Then you can publish your content. Remember you can add your website or social link in your signature

Every piece of content should have a clear call to action or a clear step in the education process so that your ideal customer moves one step closer to actually doing business with you. You can capture all this traffic onto an email list which is a tool that you will all always have access to for making sales of your products and services.

Additionally if you're growing a large social media subscriber base you're also growing your email list. That is reasonably reliable long term just in case Google decides to remove your website or Facebook decides to delete your account or YouTube becomes too competitive and so on.

Cadence and Calendar

An important aspect of planning your strategy is developing a Content calendar. This will help you visualize the amount and type of content you are going to need. Having this longer view will give you a good sense of the mix of content required to help fill any gaps.

The most important point is to pick a publishing date and then stick to it. Your customers will appreciate and expect consistency. Try mapping out a list of topics in advance and scheduling their published dates. Use a content calendar and take the time to plan out the month or week. This takes much of the guesswork out of the creation process ultimately allowing you to focus on churning out high quality content much more quickly.

For optimum results posting between one and three times a day is perfect. Three times being pretty good because that could be when somebody wakes up, when they eat lunch, and when they go to bed. Studies show this is when people look at content most often. So if you come up with those three types of times during the the day then that will be just perfect.

Then figure out a cadence. That can be a daily rhythm or a weekly rhythm. That what you know in advance what type of content you need, for the week or for the day. Then if you have your idea library, when it comes to that day it will be easy to really come up with that post off the top of your head. As opposed to thinking about that at that very moment. For example maybe you post a quote in the morning, and then you post a stat in the afternoon. Then maybe you post a video in the evening. Ideally you should have a cadence which is like a rhythm to your content marketing.

Develop your schedule template then you can use that every week as a guide. You can add to it as you go. So as cool things happen to or you come across things, take pictures of stuff, do some live videos and so on then you can add it into the mix.

Try using a tool like Hootsuite, that allows you to pre schedule your posts on all of the major social media sites. This is great because it allows you to streamline a lot of posting activities. You can pre schedule stuff, and you don't have to necessarily jump into all these platforms individually, you can simply use one tool like Hootsuite to do all this posting and analytics in once place. It also has some metrics in there that you can use from an analytical perspective, to check in on how you're doing.

Finally on a side note, stay away from any kind of blog business model that requires you to produce news content unless you're planning on creating the next TechCrunch or Huffington Post. However those sites do get the most traffic. But in that case be prepared to work crazy hours in order to cover every piece of news. For example a small news site might sometimes produce up to two hundred blog posts or individual pieces of content per day. Even if we're looking at half that number or a quarter of that number it's still a huge amount of content.

Keep focusing on your content strategy. So many times we see good content start coming out for a brand, and then it stops. What that means is they just stopped investing time in it. They stopped putting man power behind it. You need to make sure you stay consistent because you won't see tremendous growth overnight. But if you continually post content and engage with your followers then it will grow. Stick with it, keep working on and keep optimizing.

Social Media

One of the ways we can get people to be aware of our content is through posting links on social media. The economics of online content are driven by social sharing. When people share content they become advocates of it. They are standing up in a virtual way and saying I believe in this. Often times people share content not because of the content but because they love the person or the brand that's behind creating it.

Incidentally, research also shows that more than seventy percent of adult purchasing decisions are affected by what they see being shared online. In this information dense world people are paralyzed by the amount of choices and so they want to be sure of making the right decision. Some people will listen to something shared by stranger before they'll listen to your advertising or corporate marketing campaigns. For example if you find two articles where one has been shared two times and the other one has been shared two hundred and fifty times. Which one would you follow?

A lot of people do not plan their social media content and if you want to grow your platform you need to create a plan. This could be something as simple as organizing a round of tweets, a set of Instagram photos or a monthly video campaign and so on. Then do everything possible to make sure your content doesn't fall on deaf ears by choosing the platforms and content channels that your market actually uses. Discover where your market hangs out and you'll greatly improve your chances of reaching them.

Again syndicating your content across other channels is an excellent way of extending your reach to potential customers who wouldn't have otherwise heard of you. Don't be afraid to carve it up and share it across other channels and platforms. Applying a few minor tweaks to optimize and freshen up your content for different platforms will stretch your content marketing. Maybe you're not a speaker or you're not interested in getting on camera but you're a great writer. Perfect start would be to hire someone online from sites such as Fiverr or Upwork to actually speak out your written blog posts for you. Or if you do the videos yourself you can then get them transcribed into a blog post. There are many variations, just look at the previous chapter "Build Your Library" for more examples.

Brand your social media platforms. Make sure they have a really professional design, with good profile pictures, and populate all the areas of content. Your about us, include your website links, your other social links, videos and really populate all of that. Because what's going to happen is, when people are following you and liking your content. At some point they will move forward with your brand and maybe become a customer. When that happens, you want them to really be able to do that from your social platform very easily. It should be seamless for them to be able to click to your website, see your call to action, take that next step and so on. By spending some time really branding those social platforms it will ensure it's a smooth conversion funnel for your followers.

Reverse Engineer

Find social media role models in your industry that you think are doing a great job. Reverse engineer what makes them successful and think about how you can use some of their ideas as inspiration for yourself. See what's trending, what people are talking about and think about how you can apply that to your brand. People love to talk about what's popular and you can generate a buzz that way.

Take note of the fans of yours that engage with you the most on every platform. Not just friends or family. I mean people you've never met before but that are consistently interacting with you. Figure out what is attracting them to you and keep using that because it's obviously working. If you don't have that yet, then look to the people that you want to emulate and see how they are interacting with their fans.

Make sure that you stay relevant to the subject matter for your social media and your brand. People that are following you for, you know, maybe dance clothes, don't really care what you did this weekend, right? Or they don't care about pictures of your pet, they're not so interested in that. What they are interested in though is your niche and your industry. Talk about that, be an expert on that, add value to that, and that will really increase your following.

Focus on Engagement

Don't just post for the sake of posting. Make sure that every post delivers some kind of value to your followers. Otherwise, they'll stop following you and stop engaging with you. The key to all of that is delivering value. Make sure to track your results, and make adjustments accordingly as you progress. If you notice more engagement, likes and sharing, for your posts that are in the evening then maybe you should do more posts in the evening. Or perhaps adjust the times that your posts are going live. Or if you see a particular type of post that you're doing and you notice that there is not a lot of engagement then maybe you do less of those. Analyze your data and start to understand what your followers want to see. Then just give them more of what they like and less of other things they don't ;oke.

In addition to producing more engaging content you should be actively engaging with your fans. You don't want to be necessarily pushing content all the time. With social media, you should be social. Like, comment, follow other people and engage with your community. This will help you increase your brand awareness, and essentially grow your followers over time, much more quickly than if you're just pushing content. Remember to be responsive to questions, comments and reciprocate them. The more you interact in a thoughtful approachable way the more people will trust and interact with you.

Paid Content

Audience building is a huge factor when you are getting started with content marketing. There are so many people that don't have any audience. Paid advertising on social media is a great way to reach new people in your target market and attract them to your content.

While building engaging content is really powerful from an organic perspective, you can also invest in paid content. Paid advertising campaigns help to get you in front of more people, than you would be able to reach organically. Combine that with retargeting campaigns, and other things on the paid side, to really super charge your growth. Essentially it can scale things up as quickly as you want. The only criteria is that as long as you're wil ing to spend more money then you will get more traffic.

There are a number of other distinct benefits to paid advertising. The audience targeting you can achieve with advertising is so useful. You can target people by region, age, gender and specif c interests. It's a great idea to test additional filters just to make sure that you are only reaching the exact kind of audience that would be interested in your content. It's better to really focus on the exact kind of audience you want. It might be significantly smaller but it will be much more engaging. For example if we are into sportswear we might target people interested in Nike, soccer, weightlifting and the sports or other big companies in the space. Or if maybe if we are into cars we might just be deciding on audiences that are fans of the big brands.

Furthermore you can target any region that you want with paid advertising. For example if you do business in a specific city you can have your ads only show up within that city. Then you can even target the time of day. Most people aren't familiar with this and are not using this. For example if your business is only open from 8 a.m. to 5 p.m. then why would you want to pay for ads at 6 p.m? Because if someone comes to your website and they try calling you there will be no one there to answer it. The last thing you want to do is spend money during times that you're not in business.

A big goal of content marketing is to have call to actions that encourage people to take actions. It might be so that we can get them on our ema l newsletter or sign up to our website and so on. There are a lot of people who will click. The rest probably aren't going to take that call to action. So what we can do is convert this into more of a social ad unit and just show the same messaging to the people that didn't sign up on the site. Maybe they just hate pop-ups by default and they will never sign up for them. That's okay and so they might be more receptive to an advert that says subscribe or download instead of something that pops up.

The other thing we can do is start testing new messages and new content. Maybe this offer wasn't interesting to them because they don't need that guide but maybe they would be interested in your checklist instead. Or maybe they just like your email drip series that has an educational component to it. Keep testing different types of messaging just because this one wasn't valuable doesn't mean your other content isn't interesting to them. You might find that different messaging works better on social media than it does on pop-ups or banners on a website. That's one of the great benefits with social media advertising is that you can really optimize your adverts to produce the best results for the least spend.

It really is becoming increasingly difficult to stand out organically. So if you aren't using ads yet, you definitely should try.

Social Media Platforms

Each social media platform has its own uniqueness and ways of presenting content. Of course we can syndicate content across them all and we should. As mentioned before one piece of great content can be syndicated across multiple platforms and sliced up into many pieces. Pretty much all businesses are recognizing that social media is where the attention of the Internet is. Everybody's using it, but most of us don't know which platforms to use. We just need to be aware of the best practices for that. Let's take a look at some of the most popular platforms.

Facebook

With over one billion users Facebook is a powerhouse for content marketing. Content can be presented there in many different ways. From Facebook stories to posts in text, audio, video and now there are even live feeds to utilize. In fact right now Facebook is focusing on becoming more of a video centric platform with preference given to live videos. That means ranking higher in the news feed.

Experiment and be aware that the Facebook algorithm will always benefit you if you're posting content that your audience really resonates with. Facebook will always protect the end user and that is a smart business decision on their end because if people stop using it they're going to leave. Therefore they are always going to show the most relevant content to their users at the right time because that is what will keep them engaged. If they are constantly showing users ads or content from business pages then users are not going to want to engage.

Look at the posts that are getting the most engagement. The more people like, comment and share your content the higher it's going to rank. In turn the more Facebook will show your content to other fans of your page. Therefore it's very important that you are able to create content that gets engagement really quickly.

Facebook offers tools that allow you to analyze your competitors and other people in your industry. Utilize these tools to look at their content and especially the content that is performing the best. This will give you some great ideas for the type of content to focus on. Facebook is giving you these tools for a reason because they want you to become a better marketer, to engage your fan base and get the word out there. Understand what Facebook is trying to do with their platform and you will be able to leverage content a lot better.

Finally you can probably get a better result when you do that via Facebook Ads. There are over a billion people that you can reach out on Facebook using their targeting. This can help to zone in on specific audiences based on age, gender, location, employment, interests and much more.

Instagram

Instagram is another powerful tool for content marketing. It is highly addictive for its users. To stand out on one of the most popular platforms you will need to use great images, videos and design. Visually you have to capture people's attention within the first few seconds. Take shots with a professional camera if you can. Now if you have the option of editing outside of Instagram then that is a great idea.

Don't be afraid to add text over the top of images or videos. This works really well because you have very little time to grab people's attention. For example if you have a special offer that's hard to say, use text on the top. Whenever you upload a video you have the option of using a cover. Simply scroll through the entire video until you find something cool you can use.

Brand up your profile. Whatever your brand is about, make sure your name is set to suit that. When people are looking for you or your subject it will make you look like more of an authority in addition to higher search rank. Simply add in some text in there about who you are or whatever it is you do. This will give people an idea of what you're about. You may even want to jazz it up and add something funny in there or something that's unique or interesting about your brand. Also you can have a link in there to your main website, current promotion or content platform and so on.

Now that Instagram stories are here we are seeing lower engagement in the traditional feed so please take that into account and use both effectively. It's important to note that content you post in stories vs the feed will need resizing if you want it to look its best.

LinkedIn

LinkedIn is a professional oriented social network with over five hundred million users. The purpose of the website is for users to upload their business profiles, experience and qualifications there for potential employers or clients to view.

Linkedin allows users to access or post articles relevant to their business. This will help you develop a strong personal brand and build connections in your industry. Content that focuses on thought leadership or industry specific content would do well here. LinkedIn tends to be most active in the morning and afternoon as people are starting or ending their work days.

Twitter

Twitter is a short message posting application with over three hundred million users. People can write upto two hundred and forty character tweets with links or retweets of other people. It is all highly engaging and is a very active social network. However just being on Twitter isn't enough, you have to post regularly. You should be posting multiple times per day but only if you have enough content. Don't dilute it too much. You can post other status updates, photos or whatever it may be. For best results aim for posting two times a day.

Now all of your posts don't have to be promotional with links on, some can. Try to engage with the community, have conversations and reply to each other. When you reply to other people within your niche you will get more engagement. Then when you do post any links back to your site people will be more likely to click on them.

Twitter is most active around mid day. However there is no definitive formula for when to post. Use your audience personas to take an educated guess to start out, then monitor and adjust as you learn to see what works and what doesn't.

YouTube

YouTube is on fire right now with almost two billion logged in monthly users watching over an hour of content per day. It continues to innovate and is one of the best places online to be building your infuence. No matter who you are whether your a personal brand, a business or a non-profit YouTube is the place to be.

Creating content for YouTube is a breeze. Start up your camera, hit record and your well on the way. But just uploading it there and wishing for viral results won't get you far. New videos are constantly uploaded every minute of every day and so just creating content is no longer enough. When it comes to creating great content for YouTube take a look at what others in your industry are doing. This means analyzing what the most popular influencers and channels are doing then taking inspiration from that. That doesn't mean copying. Instead learn from it, put your own twist on it, improve it and make it yours.

Furthermore take inspiration from influencers outside of your niche, look at what they are doing. This again is going to provide more inspiration and ideas. If you're creating content as a means to get rich, well it's probably not going to be sustainable or enjoyable for you. But if you really believe in your content that you're sharing out there well it makes the investment much more worthwhile. In some cases you could even collaborate with people you gain inspiration from.

Now if you've been on YouTube for very long you know the power of collaboration. Whether that's teamwork, collaborating with other influencers or whether that's doing interviews with other influencers. All of these are great ways to build your influence online

Prioritize audio and video quality to ensure you create the best content for YouTube. If you have ever watched videos with bad audio or video quality you know what i'm talking about. Your probably click off them quickly. These days cameras on the average mobile phone is usually good enough to get started with. But you are going yo need need to invest in a good quality microphone. Fortunately you can afford to get a clip on lavalier mic for a minimum of one hundred dollars. It's going to make a huge difference when you hear the improved sound quality. As you grow, choose to invest in better equipment that will upgrade the quality otherwise you risk losing viewers.

Another option that you have is to use a teleprompter which can help to guide you through the script. It's up to you whether you use one or not. Regardless you're probably going to want to have some some kind of structure or notes about the content. Planning things out ahead of time and sticking to some kind of strategic structure to your content will make sure that it stays on point.

Finally, make sure that you create content that your target market would actually be interested in. Determine what people are searching for and observe which videos get the most traffic and engagement. YouTube is a social platform so be sure to engage with your audience, answer or ask questions rather than just posting videos. Try to post very second or third day. Not all of them are going to be great hits but all those individual pieces of content are adding to your subscriber base.

Hashtags

Hashtags are a user generated way to classify and sort information. They are also what people use when looking for certain types of information. When you're using a hashtag with your content you should have a reason for using that hashtag. Most people that are just getting into social media don't understand that a hashtag is a search engine in itself. Essentially it's a way to index what people are talking about and connect them with other people who are talking about the very same thing.

When you use it as a tool for connection it opens up a lot of doors for you. Your content will be getting linked to everyone else who is also using that hashtag in the search filters. Talk to others and build your relationships through mutual interests on social media through using hashtags.

While many people think hashtags are just frivolous timeline cloggers. If you use them the right way they can help to grow your audience. Really, you can find your exact audience through using proper hashtags. You can create your tweets and your postings on various sites to hit into certain hashtags or to be found by certain people. You can even use hashtags as a way to monitor what you want to achieve. But don't overdo it, some people just go buckwild with the hashtags. If you put it into too many categories you will be diluting your brand. Always think what about what you want to say with a particular message and what do you want your audience to get out of it.

Things to keep in mind when using hashtags

1. *Don't make them too long*

Don't make your readers think. Social media moves quickly so don't make your hashtag too long.

2. *Don't make them too short*

On the other hand f your tag is too short chances are it means that tag is a little ur original. A lot of people may be using that tag and so you might get lost with everybody else. For example, if you're a food blogger and you just tag food. Well everybody is tagging food, millions of users every single day. How about if you are a food blogger and you just made the most amazing cupcakes. The hashtag "artisan food" or "artisan cupcakes" might get you in with a more targeted audience.

3. *Format your hashtags*

Don't forget to format your hashtags. Capitalization helps your readers read the hashtag quicker and search engines are not case specific so don t worry.

4. *Make it Unique*

Whatever hashtag you decide to use, make sure you research it and how people are using it. Figure out if that hashtag is driving traffic or not. Because if it's not driving traffic and it doesn't have a purpose then don't use it. Brand yourself with a hashtag, use it frequently and get it into people's minds. Make the hashtag a part of your strategy, advertise that hashtag by putting it on your social media. Ideally you should make it be unique to you otherwise it's not going to be memorable and it's going to get lost. Sometimes it takes a while to come up with the right one.

Keep in mind that not all social media platforms are equal and you should not approach every social media platform in the same way. Here is an overview of how to approach each of the major platforms when using hashtags.

Facebook Hashtags

Studies have been done that show hashtags make no difference at all in your search visibility on Facebook. The main reason is that users on Facebook aren't searching for content via hashtags. So forget it when it comes to Facebook. If you really want to use them, just put in one or two maximum.

Twitter Hashtags

Tweets using one to two hashtags tend to generate the highest percentage of interaction. Using any more hashtags will likely lower engagement with that post. People want to see personal interactions and hashtags take away from that.

Instagram Hashtags

Instagram users don't mind hashtags as much. The platform lets you have up to thirty hashtags per post. Make sure to put them into the comments section so they don't look spammy and don't get in the way of your message. When you are writing out hashtags, Instagram will even autosuggest and give you statistics on the number of hashtag followers.

YouTube Hashtags

On YouTube you can use hashtags in the titles, descriptions and in the comments. Just make sure not to use over fifteen hashtags otherwise you'll be penalized. Take a look at your competitors. Visit one of their best videos, right click and then click view page source. Next click control + F and then type "keywords". This will show you all the hashtags / keywords used on that video.

Pinterest Hashtags

The thing that works here is having super unique hashtags. Maybe consider having your author or brand name as a hashtag combined with the subject matter.

Google+ Hashtags

Google+ automatically formulates hashtags that they think are suitable for your content but you can also add your own.

Writing Your Profile

Everyone has a profile these days. That could be for your business, personal brand or even a dating profile. In this case we are going to look at online business and personal brand profiles.

When someone discovers you online one of the first things they will do is to check out your profile and see what you're all about. They will be thinking about whether or not to follow you and will make up their mind on this based almost entirely on your bio. Therefore you better make sure it sounds great, engaging and compelling.

Maintain a professional tone if it is for a business profile. The goal here is to attract customers, network and establish a good reputation. Avoid using slang and focus on using professional terminology with quality checked spelling and grammar. But on the contrary make sure you avoid using too many technical words. Try not to sound smart or pompous. Aim for clarity and precision about what you do but don't make it overly fancy with buzzwords. Add in little bit of your personality for the human touch. Less is often more so be critical with your use of words and focus on shorter sentences.

Consider an imaginary person that your marketing to. Maybe even someone you really know who fits into the target audience prototype. Imagine that you are writing directly to them. Don't repeat yourself. There will be the chance to show your accomplishments later on, especially with LinkedIn. If it's for Facebook you can add in any other relevant information about your business in the additional sections. Essentially this should just be a succinct overview which informs people of who you are. That means keeping it to the essentials and avoiding covering things that will be addressed later.

The objective of your profile is to inform readers about who you are, what you have to offer them, what makes you unique and where they can discover more about you. Think about where your profile will be seen and alternate it for who will see it. For example the profile on your website will be go deeper and be more detailed than the ones on your social media accounts.

Grab attention, your first sentence needs to be great and compelling because you only have a few seconds to get your audience's attention. Begin by introducing yourself, what value your going to offer and maybe how you will solve niche relevant pain points and so on. Tell a compelling story and captivate the hearts and minds of your audience. This could be a story about your greatest accomplishments or what makes you different.

Engage them with why you are unique and how you became an authority on your topic. Include a call to action to get your audience to take the next step. For example simply sharing a link to your website or guiding them to the social media platforms you are the most active on. Or it could even be giving out a free link to a great offer that you have for them. Explain the benefits they'll receive from taking action such as a transformation or some type of achievement. Finally, wrap it up with a personal touch. Identify something personal and add in that touch that makes you more human and relatable to your audience.

Here are some examples:

"Martin feels the challenges and heartache of finding a job. For almost ten years, he has helped thousands of students learn key skills and knowledge that helps them land a dream job and rise to the top of their field."

"As a teacher, he had the honor of recruiting the best team members. Under his direction, the team has achieved and gone beyond student retention and growth goals."

"Since then, Martin has started his independent business in which he works with his clients helping them to discover careers that bring true happiness and fulfillment."

In Summary

- Make sure it sounds professional and compelling
- Add a personal touch
- Be clear and precise
- Use short sentences
- Imagine a prototypical person you're marketing to
- What makes you unique
- Capture attention, your first sentence needs to be a good one
- Start by stating who you are
- What your audience can expect from you
- How you are going to solve a particular pain point or add value
- Tell a compelling story
- Engage them with why you are unique
- Wrap it up with personality / list something personal

Content For Websites

Every fully fledged online business needs a website to stand as it's main pillar of holding content. The most important thing to consider when creating content for a website is the user experience. Optimizing for user experience includes everything from having an easy to navigate website to readable unique and conversational content. When you make the user experience the primary focus of your overall strategy conversions and audience retention will stay strong and grow.

Hold their interest and really provide value. Every element and page of your site should focus on holding your readers there or to taking actions defined by you. The content should be engaging enough to grab and hold their interest and really provide value. The longer they stay, read and engage with your website the better it looks in the eyes of Google.

When you're writing your content it's not just about the content it's also about your page. How is it laid out, is your design pretty or is it ugly? If it's ugly do you think people really want to keep looking at it? Test how it looks on a mobile device. Nowadays over fifty percent of online media is consumed on a mobile device. Therefore having a mobile-friendly website is non-negotiable.

Then, your content needs to load quickly or you risk losing readers. The slower your page loads the more frustrated your end user will be. No one wants to just sit there and wait for a website to load. Studies show that shoppers won't wait more than three seconds for a page to load when looking up a retail product. Further research has found that most people leave a site completely if they're waiting more than ten to twenty seconds for it to load. To counter that, make sure you don't have a lot of popups, scripts or things slowing down your site speed. It pays to invest in a good web designer or developer to help you with your web presence.

Keywords

When you publish a blog post or a page it does not mean that Google will automatically find it and rank it to the first place. You need to apply some specific SEO principles. Use your market research, customer persona and make use of the Google Keyword planner tool to research and find keywords. You can also make use of Google Trends to take note of any relevant trends.

Come up with a list of keywords related to your site and its content. Identify long tail keywords but if you find a shorter tail keyword with less competition then those are good too. Generally you should have a good balance between monthly searches and competition. Anything between one to ten thousand monthly searches competition is quite low. You don't want it completely too long like ten words long with only ten monthly searches. Unless it's a high-value website where you sell a big software package, real estate or some high ticket items.

Reaching The Top

More than seventy five percent of internet users never even go past the first page of search results. Reaching the top of the search results can provide massive benefits and value to your business. Now it's no cakewalk but getting a high first page ranking isn't as difficult as you might think. Coming up with a solid plan of action and following the right information will help you to reach that coveted first page ranking.

Behind every high ranking website you are guaranteed to find a solid amount of great content that helped it to achieve its high place. Realistically your content marketing and SEO efforts must work together in harmony in order for you to see any worthwhile results. Forging SEO and content together has become its own unique kind of art and strategy. Overall it's one of the most effective ways to lift your page all the way up to the top of the search engine results.

Choosing the right keywords combined with positioning them in the right places will also contribute to your search engine success. Valuable information is lucrative to being searched and shared. Afterall most people want to distribute and consume the most valuable content. Earning links to your content cements your authenticity and trust to the search engines. The more consistently you create shareable content relevant to your audience integrated with SEO principles the closer you move to mass awareness in the search engines.

SEO Principles
Format your content to be SEO friendly. Make sure your title has your main keyword in it. Then the first three lines of your description should cover the main points of the content. The first three lines of the description put it in the tags. If you add some images us the alt tags to keyword them.

Focus on creating content that is SEO friendly. Between five hundred and twelve hundred words is a good length for blog posts or a page. Anything less gives you less opportunity to include secondary keywords and your main keyword. Remember to choose a category as well. If you want a featured image make sure the featured image has the keywords in the meta description and the title as well as well as the file name.

Compliment copy with great images and you'll see more success. Visuals matter, articles with images get much more engagement than those without. but today crummy stock photos are just not going to cut it. You will need to have really good well-designed images to stand out.

Dive deeper into your content matter. Google is intensifying its focus on the quality of content. Explore topics, so instead of just quickly searching for statistic, dig a little deeper. The key for that trustworthy factor in SEO content is going to be research. The Internet has made it really easy for anyone to say anything without backing up outlandish claims so it's actually a differentiation point to go straight to an original study and pull up statistics and facts.

Be the expert, these days people value that expert / authority in content more than ever before. Reputation matters, in Google's recently updated search quality terms, the creator of that content and their history both relate to that pages rankings. For example, let's say you've been practicing your trade for ten years. Well you can position yourself as an expert with an about page that has detailed information of your career and how long you've been doing it along with dates. That will give you authority not only on SEO terms but also to your readers.

Featured Snippets
Format your online content for featured snippets. Featured snippets right now are receiving lots of attention on Google and this is likely to increase. In essence there are condensed

information blocks that literally appear in Google search results whenever someone asks Google a question. Utilize featured snippets to help you to the top spot in Google above organic results. Whenever you use formatted, numbered and bulleted lists they will actually show up in the snippets. Those usually include statistics, data or a table of contents.

Audio and Video
There is much more to content than just blogs and there is much more to search engines than Google and Bing. Incidentally audio and video content is much more easy to be found through some of the other search engines out there. iTunes or YouTube are prime examples of search engines themselves that people use on a daily basis. All it takes to rank high is to format and optimize your titles and descriptions along with relevant keywords search terms.

Usability First SEO Second
In conclusion the best strategy to reach the top is by consistently creating great content, putting it out there and building links to it. That really is all there is to it and remember the fastest way to make the search engines happy is through its users. Always remember that usability comes first and search engine optimization comes second.

Blogs

Blog posts and virality is all about conveying emotions. Who wants to read boring articles? When anything goes viral it really is all about emotions. People are either sad or happy or excited and so on. If you can evoke these emotions in people you're much more likely to have your content go viral. If you don't have any emotions in your content there's very little chance that it will go viral. Emotion is the first thing to fuel the fire. You don't always have to create sexy content to do well you just have to create content that educates or inspires people.

Think of blogs as books and organize them and structure them in a way that's readable. This also means logic and simplicity. You want your content to be logical but also simple. Remember it must be understandable.

Begin With a Title

Before you start writing any blog post always make sure you have the title written first. Most people will read your headline first and then only a few will click through and read the rest of your article. It doesn't matter how amazing your blog posts are, if you can't write a good headline no one will read the rest of your post. To help you with inspiration go to the grocery store to check out the magazines and papers. They all have great title ideas. It doesn't matter what kind of magazine they are, they all use catchy titles and that's what you need to do with your blog post. Create two or three variations and then pick the best one.

Research

Do some research on sites like Reddit, Quora and Google Trends. Just type in the terms or related terms and you can found a ton of ideas for interesting spins. There are so many interesting facts that you can identify in all niches.

Start With a Bold Statement

When you start writing your blog post you need to draw people in from the start with a bold statement. That could be some kind of groundbreaking fact or a teaser of what is inside the post later on. It's also about going over what will be discussed in the post. Essentially give them a brief overview.

The Body
Once the introduction is complete you can move onto writing the body. The body should have subheadings throughout to highlight key points or new paragraphs and subjects. Focus on readability, make it quick and easy to skim through because if people can't skim it you won't do well. Again subheadings are great way to do that and reward the reader. In addition aim to keep your paragraphs around five to seven lines maximum. Finally try to include some links out to other people because that will give more credibility for you.

The Conclusion
Towards the end you will want to wrap up your post with a solid conclusion. The purpose of the conclusion is to summarize everything about your post. In some cases you could create a cliffhanger and end your conclusion with a question or leave it open for the next time. Ending this will encourage more people to leave a comment and return to your content later on. This will increase engagement and more likely to generate sales. Don't get fancy, keep it simple.

At the end of the day it's a numbers game, you can't really predict what will go viral or not. Because if you could you'd be rich and you wouldn't even have to read this book. Keep creating blog posts and great website and then the more likely you are to go viral.

Fact Check

There is no simple magical way to have an information feed for your content that is always reliable. When you encounter information that comes from sources you don't already trust you have to be suspicious of it. In fact even when it comes from sources you do already trust you have to be a little suspicious of it. You cannot believe everything you read but that doesn't mean that you should distrust everything you read. Interrogating the information we come across online is just so important if you want to be respected for your content.

There's a very fine line between being skeptical or not easily convinced and being cynical or generally distrustful of everyone else's motives. A healthy dose of skepticism improves our critical thinking and judgment but cynicism clouds our judgment with negativity and suspicion. Logically speaking it's really difficult for any of us on a minute-by-minute basis to carefully vet the contents of every tweet or reddit post we see while we're scrolling and swiping. This work is also like any other kind of training the more you utilize your information analyzing muscles the stronger they get so we'll continue to workout.

When you review content ask yourself three questions.
1. *Who is behind this information?*
2. *What is the evidence for their claims?*
3. *What do other sources say about the organization and its claims?*

These questions are a really useful framework when you want to interpret the accuracy of information you've encountered.

Let's begin with who's behind the information. First we want to know who exactly is sharing it with you, a friend on Facebook, a stranger, a news organization? Or is it a promoted post that a company paid to insert into your feed? Then we should ask ourselves why they are sharing it. Every share has different reasons for presenting information in a particular way. Even your personal friends have motivations for sharing what they do online. They may want to signal what kind of person they are or wish to be seen as. Or they may want to win over others to their world view. or they may even be trying to get someone's attention. A journalist might be sharing information because they think it's important for their readers to know but of course that decision is based on their own personal experiences. An advocate for a particular cause might be sharing information to persuade others to join that cause.

Once you've established who is sharing the information with you and thought about why they might be doing so you can get to the heart of the matter the claim itself. Take a moment to identify any claims that are actually being made. Those could be factual claim or an opinion statement. Next you'll search for two things whether they've backed up that claim with evidence and whether that evidence is from a reliable source. Evidence could come in the form of a link to the article or study they're referencing. It could be a video or photo illustrating what they've described. It could even be the name of someone who made the claim in the first place.

The next step is to look at the source of this evidence. is it a reputable source like a trusted news organization or an expert in the field? Or is it from some random blog you've never heard of? Does it back up its claims with other sources or explain how its information was gathered? If you've never heard of the source of this information you can use a search

engine to discover what others say about it the sheer
existence of evidence

The final and really vital step. What do others say about th s
claim? Whenever you're checking on the truth you can anc
should check multiple sources to see what other information is
out there. Check a search engine or a web site known to be
an authority on the topic to see what others have published
about it. If a trustworthy source backs it up great. But if you
can't find evidence for that claim or you find evidence to the
contrary then you can be fairly certain it's not true. for
originality don't cheat but what are you bringing to this piece
that readers can't find anywhere else. what unique perspective
insider knowledge can you impart on your audience that will
make them better for reading it. if you could answer this
confidently your contents already ahead of the game.

After you have reviewed for facts you check your content
again for readability. Analyze the sentence structure,
comprehension and flow. Read it out loud and if you find that
you stumble or are find yourself lost then it's time to go over
the writing again. It might seem absurd but the level of your
writing should be at a middle school reading level if you want
to appeal to the most online readers.

Take a step back and preview the screen before you hit the
publish button. Make sure the featured image is attractive and
complements the article. Make the most of subheadings to
add structure along with bullet points to break up any lengthy
sections of text. For any visual elements make sure they dont
distract from the overall reading experience.

New Ways To Grow Your Traffic Even More

There is more to growing traffic than the conventional ways such as Google Analytics and ads. Here are some powerful tools to help get more traffic to your content.

MeetEdgar
MeetEdgar is a social sharing tool that repeatedly will share the same content over and over again. For example you create some content to share on Facebook. Most people will do that just one time. But the more you share it the more it will get seen. MeetEdgar will help you share that content multiple times and that will help to multiply your traffic.

Subscribers
Subscribers is an awesome tool to keep your audience coming back to your content. Essentially it is a push notification system that reminds people of new content, updates, activities and so on. Best of all it is free to use. Any time you have some new content use it to send out a message to your audience. Then you will get much more traffic, sales and engagement.

Ubersuggest
Enter in a keyword and Ubersuggest will give you recommendations on phrases that you should add to your content to rank higher for. You can even enter in a URL and it will disclose you how much traffic that website is receiving. This is a great way to analyze what works for your

competitors. Then you can create similar content that is much batter using the keywords they are ranking for.

Typeform
Instead of just creating content that you think is a good idea, why not ask your audience? If you just produce the content you want maybe some people will check it out. But if you go with what your audience wants then it will be a hit. Use Typeform to discover what kind of content your audience wants. Because if you produce content that your audience wants from you then the result will be more traffic.

Q Promote
This is a powerful tool that connects your content to influencers. Influencers will be linked to content that is relevant to them. Then it's a win-win both for the promoters and people creating content. Again more traffic for you.

LeadQuizzes
When people visit your website one of the most engaging things you can do is to quiz them. Quizzing people can be very engaging and at the end you can even collect their email address. Now, whenever you have some new content you can send it direct to their emails. For good examples, check out Legion Athletics, on their blog, they have a quiz in the right sidebar.

Conclusion

Bill Gates once famously declared "content is king", long before content marketing became the first choice of marketeers. In order to build brand and increase profits, businesses cannot afford to ignore content marketing.

Breaking through all the noise and getting your content out there is the biggest challenge facing content marketers today. Not only is there great content to compete with but there's also a ton of bad content crowding the way. Take a look at what everybody else is doing and then try to do it better. Now this can include just adding a little bit more to it or taking a completely different stand on it, such as being controversial. Things that are controversial tend to do better in news.

Consider the kind of content that will resonate with your audience the most. Always have them in mind and avoid sharing things that are not relevant to them. It might be tempting to share your favorite meme but if your audience is interested in higher level content then forget it. Anything else is only going to damage your following. At the end of the day all of the content you share should align with the goals, ambitions and interests of your target audience.

Dedicate the time and effort into creating quality content. Otherwise you can outsource someone to do it for you. Before you post any content always read and view it through the eyes of a consumer. The worst thing that you can do is to focus entirely on yourself. People really care mostly about their own problems and what situations they're going through. If you can provide solutions and talk to them in their terms from their perspective then that's a great thing.

Any content you share is a really an extension of who you are. Whenever you engage with your audience it gives you an opportunity to establish yourself as an authority in your field. Establishing yourself as an authority requires building trust over time through sharing the most relevant and valuable content. If you also share articles you should add your own thoughts onto it and be a curator. People value the opinion of authorities in niches.

But wait, content marketing is more than simply choosing the right content, to be effective you also need to choose the best places to share it. Never forget that content is a product that requires distribution. It's not enough to just post content on social media. Realistically you must be sure that the social media channel you use is the right platform for the content your sharing. Combine that with content of interest to your target audience and you have a winning strategy.

For example if the majority of your audience are using Instagram but your sharing mostly on Facebook then your missing out on a great opportunity to connect with them. You don't need to be on every single social media channel. Instead pick the two or three that your market engages with the most and focus your attention on those. Later on if you notice that your content on a particular social media account is lacking in engagement then focus your efforts elsewhere. Creating a target customer avatar and using it as the focus of your marketing efforts will help you to avoid marketing mistakes.

Content marketing is more than you voicing your message and opinion. It also is a conversation between you and your target audience. If you want to succeed then the opinions of your target market should be of value to you and your marketing efforts. Encourage customer feedback. For example ask your followers to share their experiences of using your products or services. Encourage the sharing of your content and ask them to tag friends who might be interested.

The best way to drive user engagement is to ask for it. It might feel weird but if you ask for likes, shares and comments then they are more likely to happen. The aim is to always influence and request engagement from your followers. Not only that but you should also seek out ways to have your followers create content for you. That could include photos of them at events of yours, product reviews, artwork and much more. Then you can share the best samples with you audience.

Maintaining an active presence on social media marketing is an effective way to stay relevant and engaging. Scheduling tools can help make sure that your posts go out on time even if you are busy with other things. The majority of social media sites offer scheduling tools that allow you to set a time and date to publish a post. In addition there are some great options to manage all of your social media scheduling, such as Hootsuite. Then you will never miss a post, you can plan the whole week out in one day.

Vary the format of your content. A common mistake is to always share the same old style of content. If your not developing and continue to just post blogs or videos without trying other forms then your missing out on more lucrative types of engagement. Experiment and try other styles. Content marketing can be incredibly versatile. One day you can share a video, the next day an interview, the next day a post and then so many more styles. The sky's the limit. Maybe one day instead of writing a complicated blog post you could hire a graphic designer to turn it into an infographic. Or maybe you can add in a little bit of a story with a write a photograph. Fundamentally you should be making a conscious effort to always vary your content.

Recognize when something isn't working and fix it. Then you will be well on your way to successful content marketing. Most people just publish and pray. They published their content and they think that it's going to magically be seen and garner critical acclaim. Track the performance of your content with analytics. Utilize the information to determine the types of content that receive the the highest levels of engagement and those which don't resonate with your audience. This will allow you to identify any weaknesses and strengths in your overall marketing strategy.

In conclusion choose your content wisely, share it appropriately and measure your results. Whenever you make the wrong choices your wasting time and money. Many content marketers make mistakes, even those who are more experienced.

If you have thoroughly read this book, taken notes and applied it then your content is ready to go to the next level. Utilizing the tips, information and strategies will set you up on a pathway to becoming an authority and a success in your niches. Any business that follows these principles will be in a leading position to engage their target audience, increase profits and grow their business.

That's not exaggerating, if you take the follow the plan take the actions and consistently evolve then your well on your way. It might take a while to see any real results but over time and with consistency you will see more shares, likes, comments and engagement than you wish. This could become a full time business for you.

However all of this will only occur if you take the right actions. All of the knowledge in this book means nothing unless you apply it. That is why I recommend you go over it once, twice or even more times until it sinks in. Revisit the chapters that you are relevant to your current situation. You can also keep up to date with the latest knowledge, tools, strategies and insights on my website.

www.wswainbrand.com

Finally i would like to say thank you for taking the time and effort to read this book. It means a lot to me that you did it. I really hope that you found some value here. It would be my pleasure if you could share this with your friends and colleagues.

Thank you and good luck!

William Swain

Bonus Chapter: Productivity Tools

There is an ever increasing gap between people who get things done versus people who are constantly distracted and lagging behind. if you want to start to improve your productivity every day it is best to develop small habits that will lead to a big impact over time.

Personal productivity is one of the smartest skills you should learn right now. This is keeping everything structured and prioritized so you're always working on the right things. Once you get into the right mindset it's time to become aware of how you are currently doing. The following tools will help you to analyze how you're spending your time.

Rescue Time
This tool automatically tracks which applications or websites you use the most. You can then see which ones are of value to you and which are not. This will make you more conscious of where you are wasting time online and in turn increase your productivity.

Toggl
Toggl is a super simple tool to track the time you're spending on specific tasks Input each task you do throughout the day and then you will start to gather metrics on where you are spending time. Ideally you want to be focused on the highest leverage activities. Anything that is below your pay rate or your not specialized in, outsource.

Pomodone
Also you can keep track of your time with the Google Chrome plug in, Pomodone. This utilizes the proven Pomodoro Technique to get your tasks done in batches of twenty five minutes. Produces extremely focused and productive work.

Workflow
A tool to make flat mind maps and expendable bullet lists. You can use on both desktop and smartphone. Make a list for every day and prioritize it.

Copy Clip

Saves time by making your clipboard history easily accessible. It keeps track of all of your latest clipboard items and makes them searchable. Extremely powerful when quickly creating content.

Text Expander

Are you typing the same text all over again? Text expander records the way you write and will save time by typing in repetitive text. Your articles will come together at a lightening speed.

Mix Max

Gmail based productivity application. It easily tracks your emails, helps scheduling meetings, email optimization and many more powerful actions through email.

Bad Habits

If Facebook is a distraction, use the news feed Eradicator. You can still use Facebook but it will replace the news feeds with some inspiring quotes. For Instagram I suggest you stay logged out and plan posts in advance with Hootsuite.

Bonus Chapter: The 90 Day Challenge

A great system to kick start your content marketing journey is a ninety day challenge. The goal is to publish one item per day every day for ninety days. This is going to do a few things for your business. Number one it will immediately get you into content creation mode. One of the biggest challenges that most people have growing a business online is the fact that they stay in consumer mode. They are focused on trying to understand how every single piece of the puzzle before engaging with the process. The irony in that is that you really can't see how all the pieces fit together until you get started because pieces that you encounter won't make sense until you've gained enough experience. Imagine driving a car from one side of America to the other. You don't need to know every single turn. All you need to know is how to get started and what turn to make on that first street.

The ninety day challenge will turn you into a consistent content creator. It's like going exercising, the first day is hard, second day it's still hard. Third day you're a little sore and it's still hard but if you stick with it for long enough you will get fit. Eventually it will become easier and more enjoyable. Then it starts to become fun and you get excited by putting out content on a regular basis. Because your seeing the growth and you realize you're being of service to your target market.

When you come from that point of being of service to your audience magical things can happen. Then you really have the opportunity to utilize the power of the search engines. Search engines always want to deliver the most valuable content to their users. For example the more videos people watch the more money YouTube can make. YouTube is going to deliver your videos more often as long as you get good numbers. Same thing with Google, if you create great content that gives Google's users a positive user experience they will begin to prioritize your content. Therefore you have to put out the best content you can.

Naturally your first content is going to be a little rough. But in order to build an audience you need to start somewhere. Anyone can start at zero and teach what they know. Little by little you begin to build that authority and an audience. You get comfortable with the process and before you know it you're a competent and excited content marketer.

I assure you that the 90 day challenge will truly help you build successful. long-term results if you stick with it. Good habits are the foundation of success. Produce content everyday for ninety consecutive days. Then continue to be of service to your audience.

Thanks for Reading!

What did you think of, **Marketing Mastery: The Ultimate Guide To Internet & Content Marketing. Drive Demand, Build a Brand, Maximize Traffic, Earn Passive Income and Sell Almost Anything**

I know you could have picked any number of books to read, but you picked this book and for that I am extremely grateful.

I hope that it added at value and quality to your everyday life. If so, it would be really nice if you could share this book with your friends and family by posting to Facebook and Twitter.

If you enjoyed this book and found some benefit in reading this, I'd like to hear from you and hope that you could take some time to post a review. Your feedback and support will help this author to greatly improve his writing craft for future projects and make this book even better.

I want you, the reader, to know that your review is very important and so, if you'd like to leave a review, all you have to do is click here and away you go. I wish you all the best in your future success!

Please keep in touch with me and updated with me at:

https://wswainbrand.com/

Thank you and good luck!

William Swain
https://wswainbrand.com/